Close Readings

Close Readings

A Course in the
Critical Appreciation of Poetry

by
A. F. SCOTT, M.A

Senior Lecturer in English,
Borough Road College of Education, Isleworth

Formerly Headmaster, the
Grammar School, Kettering

HEINEMANN
LONDON

Heinemann Educational Books Ltd
22 Bedford Square, London WC1B 3HH
LONDON EDINBURGH MELBOURNE AUCKLAND
HONG KONG SINGAPORE KUALA LUMPUR NEW DELHI
IBADAN NAIROBI JOHANNESBURG KINGSTON
EXETER (NH) PORT OF SPAIN

ISBN 0 435 18801 1
Selection and editorial matter
© A. F. Scott 1968
First published 1968
Reprinted 1969
First published as a H.E.B. paperback 1974
Reprinted 1979

Printed Offset Litho and bound in Great Britain by
Spottiswoode Ballantyne Ltd.,
Colchester and London

CONTENTS

Acknowledgements   vii

Introduction   ix

I   CLOSE READINGS

  1. Metrical Structure   3
    POEM: *Break, break, break* by Tennyson
    CRITIC: Marjorie Boulton

  2. Rhyme   8
    POEM: from *Kubla Khan* by S. T. Coleridge
    CRITIC: James Reeves

  3. Rhythm   14
    POEM: from *Nocturnall upon St Lucies Day* by John Donne
    CRITIC: H. Coombes

  4. Diction   19
    POEM: *The Habit of Perfection* by G. M. Hopkins
    CRITIC: James Reeves

  5. Metaphor/Simile   25
    POEMS: from *Psalms, XC* by Isaac Watts
           The Embankment by T. E. Hulme
    CRITICS: James Reeves
            Babette Deutsch

  6. Imagery   31
    POEMS: from *A Psalm of Life* by H. W. Longfellow
           from *The Wreck of the Deutschland* by G. M. Hopkins
           from *To his Coy Mistress* by Andrew Marvell
    CRITIC: H. Coombes

  7. Cacophony/Euphony   37
    POEM: *Popularity* by Robert Browning
    CRITIC: Lascelles Abercrombie

  8. Connection through Imagery   42
    POEM: *To Autumn* by John Keats
    CRITIC: Reuben Arthur Brower

9. Generalization/Concrete particularity   48
   PASSAGES: from *Richard II* and *Troilus and Cressida* by
      Shakespeare
   CRITIC: L. C. Knights

10. Consistency of impression   53
    POEM: from *Hyperion* by John Keats
    CRITIC: C. Day Lewis

11. Poetic Thought   57
    POEM: *A Poison Tree* by William Blake
    CRITIC: H. Coombes

12. Accurate Observation   65
    POEM: *Consider* by W. H. Auden
    CRITIC: A. Alvarez

13. Range in Imagery, Sound, Tone, Ironies   72
    POEM: from *Epistle IV, Of the Use of Riches* by Alexander
       Pope
    CRITIC: Reuben Arthur Brower

14. Symbolic Image   78
    POEM: *A Sonnet* by George Barker
    CRITIC: C. Day Lewis

15. Personal Feeling   82
    POEM: *Do Not Go Gentle Into That Good Night* by
       Dylan Thomas
    CRITIC: Archibald MacLeish

II PASSAGES FOR CLOSE READING
   With Questions   93
   Without Questions   110

ACKNOWLEDGEMENTS

The Author and Publishers wish to thank the following for permission to reprint copyright material:

L. C. Knights, Cambridge University Press and Chatto & Windus Ltd for extracts from *Scrutiny*, Vol. III, No. 2, September 1934, reprinted in *Explorations*; Archibald MacLeish and The Bodley Head for an extract from *Poetry and Experience*; Oxford University Press, Inc. for two extracts from *The Fields of Light* by Reuben Arthur Brower; Chatto & Windus Ltd for three extracts from *Literature and Criticism* by H. Coombes and an extract from *The Shaping Spirit* by A. Alvarez; Lascelles Abercrombie and Martin Secker & Warburg for an extract from *The Theory of Poetry*; James Reeves for three extracts from *Understanding Poetry*; Cecil Day Lewis and Jonathan Cape Ltd for two extracts from *The Poetic Image*; John Johnson for an extract from *The Anatomy of Poetry* by Marjorie Boulton; Babette Deutsch and Curtis Brown Ltd for an extract from *Poetry in Our Time*; the Trustees for the Copyrights of the late Dylan Thomas and J. M. Dent & Sons Ltd for 'Do Not Go Gentle Into That Good Night' (from *Collected Poems*); Ruth Pitter and The Cresset Press Ltd for 'The Viper'; Louis MacNeice and Faber and Faber Ltd for 'Meeting Point' (from *Collected Poems*); W. H. Auden and Faber and Faber Ltd for 'Consider' (from *Collected Shorter Poems 1927–1957*); Thom Gunn and Faber and Faber Ltd for 'Autumn Chapter in a Novel' (from *The Sense of Movement*); Philip Larkin and Faber and Faber Ltd for 'Mr Bleaney' (from *The Whitsun Weddings*); Oxford University Press for 'Inversnaid', 'The Starlight Night', 'The Habit of Perfection' and an extract from 'The Wreck of the Deutschland' (from *Poems of Gerard Manley Hopkins*); W. R. Rodgers and Martin Secker & Warburg Ltd for 'Beagles' (from *Awake! and other Poems*); the Estate of the late Mrs Frieda Lawrence and Laurence Pollinger Ltd for an extract from 'Fish' by D. H. Lawrence; Elizabeth Jennings and David Higham Associates Ltd for 'Old Woman' (from *A Sense of the World*); the Trustees of the Hardy Estate and Macmillan & Co Ltd for 'Afterwards' (from *The Collected Poems of Thomas Hardy*); Peter Redgrove and Routledge & Kegan Paul for 'Ghosts' (from *The Nature of Cold Weather*).

INTRODUCTION

A whole attitude to poetry lies behind the title *Close Readings*. For poetry can communicate the actual quality of experience 'with a subtlety and precision unapproachable by any other means'. We can only share this experience by an appreciation of the words, for it is the words which stand for all that the poet has felt, for all that has passed through his imagination. Although poetry and prose both use words, prose uses chiefly the meaning, whereas poetry uses *all* the qualities of words. It is for this reason, therefore, that poetry calls for 'close readings'.

The supreme importance of the words of the poet demands particular analysis, and what better than to turn to examples of good practice in this difficult task.

Examples of good practice form the main, solid part of this book. These take the form of close readings by major critics of poems and passages of poetry which are quoted in each essay. These essays are carefully selected and arranged to fit into a clear teaching plan, which is to present different aspects of poetic expression (metrical structure, rhyme, rhythm, diction, imagery, tone), different problems of interpretation, different forms of critical analysis. The essays move from the simplest aspects to the more profound.

The exciting ideas in the critical essays will, perhaps, be strange to many students, who will need help before they can make these ideas their own. Hence I have given brief supplements in the relevant places on such things as metre, modes of metaphor, imagery, ambiguity, symbolism and concrete particularity. This practice is extended to include concepts such as the poet's 'conscious and unconscious purpose' spoken of by James Reeves in relation to the sound effects in *Kubla Khan*. Whenever a concept is complicated, drawing on a different and unexplored area of knowledge, first it has been briefly explained, and then put forward as a topic for discussion and enquiry. This part of the course, with the supplementary information on literary terms and technical vocabulary, is intended to give students tools of the art of close reading comparable to those the critics themselves are using.

The critics often take for granted a background knowledge of

literary techniques and aspects of analysis, so—where relevant—
books and essays are mentioned for further reading.

The working part of the book is strengthened by the inclusion
of suitable poems to follow each critical essay. Questions on these
poems are precise and so worded as to give reasonable practice on
the important issues raised in the immediately preceding analysis.
Throughout, the questions are intended to be positive and helpful,
leading the student to the approach to be made to each poem, and
also concentrating on the full meaning of the text.

The last section consists of a number of poems and passages
chosen for close reading. These poems give the opportunity to
display the sensibility, discrimination and judgment which good
criticism demands, and should prove useful to students in sixth
forms, colleges of education and universities.

A. F. SCOTT

I
Close Readings

A series of critical extracts illustrating different aspects of poetry, with editorial commentaries and exercises in practical criticism

1. METRICAL STRUCTURE

POEM: *Break, break, break* by Tennyson.
CRITIC: Marjorie Boulton.

We must begin by making a distinction between rhythm and metre. Both words, when used concerning English poetry, refer to the pattern of stresses. Rhythm I take as meaning every possible aspect of this; metre as meaning the symmetrical, repetitive pattern of stresses. Rhythm thus includes metre but metre is a relatively small part of rhythm. The metre of poetry is the basic pattern of stressed and unstressed syllables.

Here is Tennyson's *Break, break, break* with the lines numbered for easy reference later:

1 Break, break, break

2 On thy cold gray stones, O sea!

3 And I would that my tongue could utter

4 The thoughts that arise in me.

5 O well for the fisherman's boy,

6 That he shouts with his sister at play!

7 O well for the sailor lad,

8 That he sings in his boat on the bay!

9 And the stately ships go on,

10 To their haven under the hill;

11 But O for the touch of a vanished hand

12 And the sound of a voice that is still!

3

13 Breák, breák, breák,

14 At the foot of thy crágs, O Séa!

15 But the ténder gráce of a day that is déad

16 Will never come báck to me.

We can probably hear a pattern in this poem long before we can say what the basic metre is. It is necessary to read the poem aloud, intelligently, and mark the syllables that are naturally stressed, remembering that equal stress is not laid on all stressed syllables.

The basic metre of this poem is anapaestic, strange as this may seem in view of its slow, melancholy rhythm. Completely regular anapaestic trimeters are found in lines 6, 8 and 12, and nearly regular ones with only one unstressed syllable missing in lines 5, 10 and 14. Lines 11 and 15 also have unmistakably the anapaestic beat, but each, a tetrameter, has at least one iambic foot. Eight puzzling lines remain: the two pathetic repetitions of 'Break, break, break . . .' would read as three almost equal strong stresses, making a very heavy line for the mood of mourning. Lines 2, 4, 7 and 16 have each three stresses, with a mixture of iambic and anapaestic feet. The effect of these complicated variations is to give a faltering effect to the poem, which well suggests by its sound the emotion it portrays.

from *The Anatomy of Poetry*

COMMENTARY

Metre, formerly called measure, is determined by the type and number of feet in a line of verse. Analysis of the metre is called scansion. A unit in the scansion of verse (in English poetry) is one strong stress or accent.

The most commonly used feet are as follows:

Iambus	�‿	´	defeát
Trochee	´	�‿	émptў
Anapaest	˿	˿ ´	serenáde
Dactyl	´	˿ ˿	mérrilў

Occasional feet are:

Spondee   ˊ ˊ
Pyrrhic   �‿ �‿
Amphibrach   �‿ ˊ �‿

Examples

Iambic: The cúr|fĕw tólls| thĕ knéll| of párt|ĭng dáy|

Trochaic: Eárth, rĕ|ceíve ăn| hónoŭred| gué͝st;

       Wílliăm| Yéats ĭs| laíd tŏ| rést.

Anapaestic: Thĕre ăre mán|y̆ whŏ sáy| thăt ă dóg| hăs hĭs dáy|

Dactylic: Mérrĭly̆| mérrĭly̆| shăll Ĭ líve| nów.

The metre of poetry is determined by the number of feet in the line. The following names are used: monometer, one foot; dimeter, two feet; trimeter, three feet; tetrameter, four feet; pentameter, five feet; hexameter, six feet; heptameter, seven feet; octameter, eight feet.

Rhyme Schemes

(a) Heroic Couplet
    Iambic pentameter, rhyming in couplets.

(b) Octosyllabic Couplet
    Iambic tetrameter, rhyming in couplets.

(c) Iambic Hexameter
    Used with pentameters to avoid monotony.

Iambic Pentameter Stanzas

(a) Quatrain, four-line stanza, rhyming *abab*.

(b) Sextain, six-line stanza, rhyming *ababcc*.

(c) Septet, seven-line stanza; Rhyme Royal or Chaucerian Heptastich; rhyming *ababbcc*.

(d) Octave, eight-line stanza; Ottava Rima; rhyming *abababcc*.

(e) Spenserian Stanza, nine-line stanza, rhyming *ababbcbcc*, last line an Alexandrine.

Sonnet

  (*a*) Italian. Octave *abba, abba*; Sestet *cdc, dcd*; or *cde, cde*.

  (*b*) English or Shakespearean. *abab, cdcd, efefgg*.

  (*c*) Miltonic
     Follows Italian (or Petrarchan sonnet) but no division between octave and sestet.

Consult Babette Deutsch, *A Poetry Handbook*.

PRACTICAL CRITICISM

1. Scan the following passages, divide the lines into feet, mark the stressed syllables throughout, and name the kind of feet.

  (*a*) There Honour comes, a pilgrim grey,
     To bless the turf that wraps their clay;
     And Freedom shall a while repair,
     And dwell, a weeping hermit there.

  (*b*) How commentators each dark passage shun,
     And hold their farthing candle to the sun.

  (*c*) I am out of humanity's reach,
     I must finish my journey alone,
     Never hear the sweet music of speech,
     I start at the sound of my own.

  (*d*) The party 'gainst the which he doth contrive
     Shall seize one half his goods; the other half
     Comes to the privy coffer of the state.

  (*e*) She hurried at his words, beset with fears,
     For there were sleeping dragons all around,
     At glaring watch, perhaps, with ready spears;—
     Down the wide stairs a darkling way they found.
     In all the house was heard no human sound.
     A chain-droop'd lamp was flickering by each door;
     The arras, rich with horseman, hawk and hound,
     Flutter'd in the besieging wind's uproar;
     And the long carpets rose along the gusty floor.

2. Discuss the following in the light of (i) the metre of the verse; (ii) the use of language; (iii) the theme:

(*a*) We have strict statutes and most biting laws,
  The needful bits and curbs to headstrong weeds,
  Which for this fourteen years we have let slip;
  Even like an o'er-grown lion in a cave,
  That goes not out to prey. Now, as fond fathers,
  Having bound up the threat'ning twigs of birch,
  Only to stick it in their children's sight
  For terror, not to use, in time the rod
  Becomes more mock'd than fear'd; so our decrees,
  Dead to infliction, to themselves are dead,
  And liberty plucks justice by the nose;
  The baby beats the nurse, and quite athwart
  Goes all decorum.

Shakespeare, Measure for Measure

(*b*) Avenge, O Lord, thy slaughter'd saints, whose bones
  Lie scatter'd on the Alpine mountains cold;
  Ev'n them who kept thy truth so pure of old,
  When all our fathers worshipped stocks and stones,
  Forget not: in thy book record their groans
  Who were thy sheep, and in their ancient fold
  Slain by the bloody Piedmontese that roll'd
  Mother with infant down the rocks. Their moans
  The vales redoubled to the hills, and they
  To Heav'n. Their martyr'd blood and ashes sow
  O'er all th' Italian fields, where still doth sway
  The triple Tyrant; that from these may grow
  A hundred-fold, who, having learn'd thy way,
  Early may fly the Babylonian woe.

Milton, On the Late Massacre in Piedmont

(*c*)   He has outsoared the shadow of our night;
  Envy and calumny and hate and pain,
  And that unrest which men miscall delight,
  Can touch him not and torture not again;
  From the contagion of the world's slow stain
  He is secure, and now can never mourn
  A heart grown cold, a head grown gray in vain;
  Nor, when the spirit's self has ceased to burn,
With sparkless ashes load an unlamented urn.

Shelley, Adonais

2. RHYME

POEM: *Kubla Khan* by S. T. Coleridge.
CRITIC: James Reeves.

> In Xanadu did Kubla Khan
> A stately pleasure-dome decree:
> Where Alph, the sacred river, ran
> Through caverns measureless to man
> Down to a sunless sea.

This clearly announces a magical experience of profound significance, and by its sheer sound qualities it produces in the reader
that 'willing suspension of disbelief' which Coleridge described
as the prerequisite to the enjoyment of poetry. Look more closely
at these five lines of Coleridge, you will see that part of the sound
quality of the lines comes from the rhyme-scheme: lines 1, 3 and 4
rhyme with each other; line 2 rhymes with line 5. It is not necessary to define rhyme; everyone can recognize it. In traditional
poetry, composed to be sung or spoken, rhyme was not always
exact; written poetry demands a close approximation to exactness.
In the five lines we are examining exact rhyme only occurs if we
pronounce 'Khan' to rhyme with 'man'. I think Coleridge meant
it to be so pronounced: it seems to me more satisfying that way.
The reason for this is that, not only is there a rhyme at the end of
the line, there is also an internal rhyme: in fact, a pair of internal
rhymes, which create an almost musical effect. 'Xan-' rhymes with
'Khan', and '-du' with 'Ku-'. Say the line aloud and you will
instantly hear what I mean. This first line seems, then, to do two
things: it directs your mind to the legendary oriental conqueror
who was noted for his power and the splendour of his creations;
it suggests also that the experience you are to share in is one of
profound magical significance. I am not concerned here with the
question how far this was Coleridge's purpose; I hardly think that
matters. I am inclined to think that his purpose was unconscious;
otherwise it might not have been so successful: we are all too
familiar with the too deliberate efforts of some poets to create a
magical atmosphere.

8

Other sound-effects can hardly be missed, even on a silent reading of the lines. In each of the five lines there is a pair of words beginning with the same sound: 'Kubla' and 'Khan'; 'dome' and 'decree'; 'river' and 'ran'; 'measureless' and 'man'; 'sunless' and 'sea'. Was this accidental? I can hardly think so. But if it is deliberate, it is very artfully and subtly done, so as not to obtrude itself. Do you not feel, as I do, that when Tennyson composes word-music, as he so often does, his art does not sufficiently conceal itself, and we are aware of its artificiality?

> Sweeter thy voice, but every sound is sweet;
> Myriads of rivulets hurrying thro' the dawn,
> The moan of doves in immemorial elms,
> And murmuring of innumerable bees.

If a writer produces these effects consciously, with deliberate artifice, we are entitled to call him a good craftsman, a skilful versifier; only if he has much more to offer us can we call him a true poet. A true poet is likely to produce his effects without the air of self-consciousness. Keats said that 'If poetry comes not as naturally as leaves to a tree, it had better not come at all'. At the same time, unless there is a long tradition behind a poet, there is likely to be a need for conscious effort, even for a degree of artificiality. This at any rate is the impression we get from what is called alliterative verse.

from *Understanding Poetry*

COMMENTARY

James Reeves speaks of Coleridge's 'unconscious purpose' regarding the first line of *Kubla Khan,* which does direct our mind to the legendary oriental conqueror and suggests that what we are about to share in is one of profound magical significance. Were this Coleridge's *conscious* purpose, he would concentrate on the sound of the words, and might, by working at this surface level, lose the true individual quality of thought and feeling expressed. He would be more a versifier than a true poet, who must fuse meaning, sound, associations into a unity, and here the poet's purpose would not be conscious or deliberate.

Reeves later draws our attention to Tennyson's word-music,

where art does not sufficiently conceal itself and so we see its artificiality. In the quotation from Tennyson we see the skill or craft of *making* word-music. This reminds us of what Sir Philip Sidney said, 'It is not riming and versing that maketh a Poet, no more than a long gowne maketh an Advocate, who though he pleaded in armour should be an Advocate and no Souldier.'

Take 'the conscious and unconscious purpose of a poet' as the subject for a discussion.

At the end of his account of Kubla Khan, Reeves refers to 'a long tradition behind a poet . . .' 'Tradition and the Individual Talent' by T. S. Eliot is an illuminating essay on this subject.

Rhyme or *Rime* (Greek *rhuthmós,* Latin *rhythmus,* measured motion) is identity of sound between two words, considered from the last fully accented vowel to the end of the word, as in *hair, fair*; or *state, relate*; or *equality, frivolity.* The identity of sound must not include the consonant coming before the last accented vowel: *feet* and *defeat* is not a true rhyme.

There are various kinds of rhyme:

(1) Masculine rhyme is rhyme of one syllable, as in *last, cast.*
(2) Feminine or double is rhyme of two syllables, the second being unstressed, as in *older, colder.*
(3) Triple rhyme, stressed syllable followed by two unstressed ones as in *glorious, victorious.*
(4) Middle, medial or internal rhyme is rhyme coming in the middle as well as at the end of the same line of verse:

> And I laugh to see them whirl and flee,
> Like a swarm of golden bees.

(5) Eye rhyme is imperfect rhyme: the two words from the spelling look as though they should rhyme but do not (e.g. *love, move*; *bough, rough, cough*).
(6) Identical rhyme. This term stands for the repetition of the same word in the rhyming position, so used for emphasis. Keats uses it in *Isabella*:

> All close they met again, before the dusk
> Had taken from the stars its pleasant veil,
> All close they met, all eves, before the dusk
> Had taken from the stars its pleasant veil.

The reference above to traditional poetry implies knowledge of the ballad (Latin *ballare,* to dance). This was originally a song accompanied by a dance. Later the name was applied to a narrative poem. This was anonymous, drawn from legend and folk tales. It was sung by the minstrels to their own accompaniment. Ballads were passed down by word of mouth from generation to generation. They were direct and simple, with romantic, historical or supernatural settings.

Chevy Chase, Sir Patrick Spens and *Clerk Saunders* are well-known examples of true medieval ballads.

See M. J. C. Hodgart, *The Ballads*
    G. H. Gerould, *The Ballad of Tradition.*

PRACTICAL CRITICISM

1. What are the main characteristics of the Ballads? Illustrate from several you have read.

2. What do the Ballads tell us of the 'direct and intimate collaboration of poet and audience in the art of oral poetry'?

3. In the first two passages below comment on the following:

    (i) the poet's use of rhyme in order to gain particular effects.

    (ii) the effect of rhyme on the general sound of the passage.

    (iii) the connection between sound and meaning or intention.

4. Comment on this couplet in (*b*):

> Lightly they frolic o'er the vacant mind,
> Unenvied, unmolested, unconfined.

5. Comment on passages (*c*) and (*d*), showing by what **device** Butler and Byron make rhyme comic.

(*a*) Calm was the day, and through the trembling air a
     Sweet-breathing Zephyrus did softly play b
     A gentle spirit, that lightly did delay b
     Hot Titan's beams, which then did glister fair; a
     When I (whom sullen care, a

Through discontent of my long fruitless stay b
In Prince's court, and expectation vain   c
Of idle hopes, which still do fly away, b
Like empty shadows, did afflict my brain.) c
Walked forth to ease my pain. c
Along the shore of silver streaming Thames; d
Whose rutty bank, the which his river hems, d
Was painted all with variable flowers, e
And all the meads adorned with dainty gems d
Fit to deck maidens' bowers e
And crown their paramours e
Against the bridal day, which is not long: f
    Sweet Thames! run softly, till I end my song. f

Spenser, Prothalamion

(b) Yes! let the rich deride, the proud disdain, a
These simple blessings of the lowly train; a
To me more dear, congenial to my heart, b
One native charm, than all the gloss of art; b
Spontaneous joys, where Nature has its play, c
The soul adopts, and owns their first-born sway; c
Lightly they frolic o'er the vacant mind, d
Unenvied, unmolested, unconfined: d
But the long pomp, the midnight masquerade, e
With all the freaks of wanton wealth array'd, e
In these, ere triflers half their wish obtain, f
The toiling pleasure sickens into pain; f
And, e'en while fashion's brightest arts decoy, g
The heart distrusting asks, if this be joy. g

Goldsmith, The Deserted Village

(c) He was in Logick a great Critick,
Profoundly skill'd in Analytick.
He could distinguish, and divide
A Hair 'twixt South and South-West side:
On either which he would dispute,
Confute, change hands, and still confute.
He'd undertake to prove by force
Of Argument, a Man's no Horse.
He'd prove a Buzard is no Fowl,
And that a Lord may be an Owl,

A Calf an *Alderman,* a Goose a *Justice,*
And Rooks *Committee-men,* and *Trustees;*
He'd run in Debt by Disputation,
And pay with Ratiocination.
All this by Syllogism, true
In mood and Figure, he would do.

Butler, *Hudibras*

(*d*) Some women use their tongues—she *look'd* a lecture,
Each eye a sermon, and her brow a homily,
An all-in-all sufficient self-director,
Like the lamented late Sir Samuel Romilly,
The Law's expounder, and the State's corrector,
Whose suicide was almost an anomaly—
One sad example more, that 'All is vanity'—
(The jury brought their verdict in 'Insanity'.)

Byron, *Don Juan*

3. RHYTHM

POEM: *Nocturnall upon St Lucies Day* by John Donne.
CRITIC: H. Coombes.

Now here is the first stanza of Donne's 'Nocturnall upon St Lucies Day, being the shortest day':

> Tis the yeares midnight, and it is the dayes,
> *Lucies,* who scarce seaven houres herself unmaskes,
> The Sunne is spent, and now his flasks
> Send forth light squibs, no constant rayes;
>   The worlds whole sap is sunke:
> The generall balme th' hydroptique earth hath drunk,
> Whither, as to the beds-feet, life is shrunke,
> Dead and enterr'd; yet all these seeme to laugh,
> Compar'd with mee, who am their Epitaph.

The feeling that inspires the poem is one of loss and profound dejection at the death of his lover; and it is apparent from the start that we are dealing with something very different from the ordinary run of mournful love-poems. The poet is writing at midnight on the shortest day of the year; the sun's strength at this season appears only in intermittent feeble gleams; all the sap and moisture of plants and trees has sunk back into the huge water-swollen earth; the agents of life (for instance, flowers) have shrivelled and died; yet the gloom of none of these things can compare with that of the poet, whose heavy task it is to consider and record their fate. Such is, briefly, the prose-content of the stanza, a content which we shall find to be superbly fused with and given emotional force by the rhythmical expression.

Now what is it that we feel immediately in the movement of this poetry? It is not incantatory. If you tried to reduce the movement of this verse to anything like incantation you would produce ridiculous effects. But read it as the poet has written it, giving attention to the stresses and pauses, you will feel the power of rhythm to convey and reinforce the emotion and thought-content of the words. The first line is very quiet, the lack of emphasis suggesting the low spirit of the poet, though there is something quietly solemn even in that colourless second part of the line. Then the voice comes down on 'Lucies' with more weight, stressing it: in addition to giving the name of this day which is so full of significance for the poet, Donne wishes to convey the hint of irony that he feels in the word, which has connections in his mind with 'lucid' and 'lucent': the atmosphere and temper of the tune is anything but that to Donne. The slow and laborious movement of 'who scarce seaven houres', coming after the comma and pause, reproduces a sense of difficulty and obstruction in the sun's efforts to appear; there is for the poet no bright energy in nature's operations at this season. The very source of life is 'spent' (later in the poem, we feel an added intensity in this thought when the poet states that his own sun, the lost one, can never renew itself). The fourth line is remarkable in that every word receives emphasis, every syllable except one: but note the thin sounds in the rather contemptuous phrase 'light squibs' as against the sure broad vowels of 'no constant rayes': the heavy 'no', with 'rayes', especially emphasizes the lifeless and negative quality of despair, despair that is in this instance deep and understood, not mild and incoherent. The fifth line is extremely slow and heavy with the poet's spirit and with the sodden weight of the earth. There is some quickening in lines six and seven as the poet gives an image of the thirsty earth, absorbing everything inevitably; but then fall the three heavy words 'shrunke', 'dead' and 'enterr'd', words of such intense meaning in the poet's imagination, for they refer to a loved person's body as well as to the general 'life' of natural things at this season. After this solemnity there is a lighter movement rising to the unexpected word 'laugh', and passing into an easy but deliberate conversationalism in 'Compar'd with mee'. Then the last four words resume the steady inevitability. The emphasis on the tiny word 'am' is not only to indicate the certainty of the fact that he is the epitaph, the recorder of these melancholy things; it also gives greater point to the paradox of his being the worst-off of all although he is still alive—I AM, they are NOT, and yet I am in a worse state than they.

A full analysis of the stanza would of course reveal further profundity and wealth of meaning; I have restricted myself to its rhythm as far as was possible (and have not examined, for instance, the significance of words like 'flasks,' 'whole', 'hydroptique', and the ambiguity of 'light', and of that sudden, surprising simile 'as to the beds-feet'). And the essential point that emerges is this: that Donne does not use rhythm as a musical attraction that is likely to confuse or lessen the significance of what he is saying .He is not more concerned with the 'how' than with the 'what': all is one in Donne. The movement follows the direction of the emotion and the thought; it is not imposed rigidly and as it were ready-made on the material: it seems to rise inevitably out of the poet's feeling and attitude. It is organic, not separable; living and varied, not mechanical. It is the reverse of sing-song in that it is based on the flexibility of the living spoken language. And ultimately this functional rhythm has a far deeper and finer and more complex 'music' than any incantation can provide.

from *Literature and Criticism*

COMMENTARY

Rhythm (Greek *rhuthmós*, measured motion) is the measured flow of words and phrases in verse or prose. There is the rhythm achieved by the ordinary arrangement of stressed and unstressed syllables, producing something more or less mechanical, such as these lines by Macaulay in *Ivry*:

'The King is come to marshal us, in all his armour drest,
And he has bound a snow-white plume upon his gallant crest.
He looked upon his people, and a tear was in his eye;
He looked upon the traitors, and his glance was stern and high.
Right graciously he smiled on us, as rolled from wing to wing,
Down all our line, a deafening shout, "God save our Lord the King".'

Here the rhythm is external, and made to fit a selected pattern.

Now let us apply to other poets what Coombes has said above of Donne.

In more complex poetry the rhythm is organic, and is part of the process in creating the poem. The poet who has been deeply moved is now translating the experience into an artistic form through the medium of words. These words will give substance to his thought and feelings and to the images which give the emotional colouring to those thoughts and feelings. Though the poet may be shaping the poem to conform to some established verse pattern, he will also make the words conform to the flow of his feelings. The rhythm of the line will follow the very rhythm of his own feelings, the organic rhythm will be created, and as this is individual the poem will not repeat the exact rhythm of a fixed metre, but have the individual mark of the poet upon it.

Complexity of rhythm is shown in the following lines from Shakespeare's Sonnet 73.

> That time of year thou mayst in me behold
> When yellow leaves, or none, or few, do hang
> Upon those boughs which shake against the cold,
> Bare ruin'd choirs where late the sweet birds sang.
> In me thou seest the twilight of such day
> As after sunset fadeth in the west,
> Which by and by black night doth take away,
> Death's second self, that seals up all in rest.

PRACTICAL CRITICISM

1. Indicate the differences in the use of rhythm in the following passage:

> The night is chill; the forest bare;
> Is it the wind that moaneth bleak?
> There is not wind enough in the air
> To move away the ringlet curl
> From the lovely lady's cheek—
> There is not wind enough to twirl
> The one red leaf, the last of its clan,
> That dances as often as dance it can,
> Hanging so light, and hanging so high,
> On the topmost twig that looks up at the sky.

> > Coleridge, *Christabel*

2. 'The movement follows the direction of the emotion and the thought.' Discuss, with close reference to this passage.

> And there lay the rider distorted and pale,
> With the dew on his brow, and the rust on his mail:
> And the tents were all silent, the banners alone,
> The lances unlifted, the trumpet unblown.

And the widows of Ashur are loud in their wail,
And the idols are broke in the temple of Baal;
And the might of the Gentile, unsmote by the sword,
Hath melted like snow in the glance of the Lord!

Byron, *The Destruction of Sennacherib*

3. Analyse and discuss the effects of rhythm paying special
attention to the words and phrases in italics.

There lies the port: the vessel *puffs her sail*:
There *gloom the dark broad seas*. My mariners,
Souls that have toil'd, and wrought, and thought with me—
That ever with a *frolic welcome* took
The thunder and the sunshine, and opposed
Free hearts, free foreheads—you and I are old;
Old age hath yet his honour and his toil;
Death closes all: but something ere the end,
Some work of noble note, may yet be done,
Not unbecoming men that strove with Gods.
The *lights begin to twinkle* from the rocks:
The *long day wanes*: the *slow moon climbs*: the deep
Moans round with many voices. Come, my friends,
'Tis not too late to seek a newer world.

Tennyson, *Ulysses*

4. Write a short appraisal of the rhythmic effects, and their
relationship with Longfellow's central theme.

Thus the Birch Canoe was builded
In the valley, by the river,
In the bosom of the forest;
And the forest's life was in it,
All its mystery and its magic,
All the lightness of the birch-tree,
All the toughness of the cedar,
All the larch's supple sinews;
And it floated on the river
Like a yellow leaf in Autumn,
Like a yellow water-lily.

Longfellow, *Hiawatha*

4. DICTION

POEM: *The Habit of Perfection* by Gerard Manley Hopkins.
CRITIC: James Reeves.

As a young man, Gerard Manley Hopkins was a fervent admirer
of Keats. It was partly through Keats's poems that he realized the
appeal of the world of sense. The great decision he made was to
renounce the world of sense in favour of a life of self-denial,
austerity and spiritual self-perfection. This momentous act of
renunciation he celebrated in *The Habit of Perfection*, in some ways
his finest poem.

> Elected Silence, sing to me
> And beat upon my whorlèd ear,
> Pipe me to pastures still and be
> The music that I care to hear.
>
> Shape nothing, lips; be lovely-dumb:
> It is the shut, the curfew sent
> From there where all surrenders come
> Which only makes you eloquent.
>
> Be shellèd, eyes, with double dark
> And find the uncreated light:
> This ruck and reel which you remark
> Coils, keeps, and teases simple sight.
>
> Palate, the hutch of tasty lust,
> Desire not to be rinsed with wine:
> The can must be so sweet, the crust
> So fresh that comes in fasts divine!
>
> Nostrils, your careless breath that spend
> Upon the stir and keep of pride,
> What relish shall the censers send
> Along the sanctuary side!

O feel-of-primrose hands, O feet
That want the yield of plushy sward,
But you shall walk the golden street
And you unhouse and house the Lord.

And, Poverty, be thou the bride
And now the marriage feast begun,
And lily-coloured clothes provide
Your spouse not laboured-at nor spun.

Hopkins was preparing, not only to become a member of the
Roman Church, but also a priest and a Jesuit—entailing the triple
vow of poverty, chastity and obedience. That his conversion was
no simple intellectual decision but a total act of renunciation is
evidenced in the poem; he uses his marvellous command of
sensuous imagery for the purpose of making his renunciation of
the life of sense. It is as if he said, 'Do not imagine that this world
is nothing to me—it is everything I have known; but it is not
enough.' The denial of the senses is, paradoxically, an even more
exquisite exercise of sensuous delight. Silence is more beautiful
than any sound, beautiful as sound can be; the 'uncreated light'
of spiritual illumination is more beautiful than the manifold and
confusing appearances of the world of nature; fasting is more
satisfying than the lust of the palate; the smell of incense has more
relish than the casual satisfactions of the nostrils; self-denial is to
give a keener, subtler and more profound delight than all the
delights of self-indulgence. This is, in brief, the meaning of the
poem: but it is not the poem. The poem is to be apprehended,
not by the intellect alone but also, and mainly, by the senses. In
this way the reader realizes, not only the nobility of Hopkins's
resolution, but also its pathos.

In this poem you will have noticed words such as 'elected',
'whorlèd', 'curfew', 'surrenders', 'eloquent', 'shellèd', 'uncreated',
'relish', 'censers', 'sanctuary', 'sward' and 'spouse'. This is in some
ways a strange choice of words. This choice is called a poet's
diction, and nothing is a clearer indication of a poet's interests and
habit of mind than his diction. From the diction of this poem you
would gather, correctly, that Hopkins was a man interested in
literature and the scriptures. The use of words like 'thou' and
'shellèd' indicates a literary turn of mind; while a number of
expressions reveal a close familiarity with the Bible.

Of other poets' diction we may say that it is plain or ornate, homely or exotic, colloquial or literary, up-to-date or archaic. Each kind of diction has its attractions and its dangers. Excessively colloquial language degenerates into slang and vulgarity; excessively high-flown and literary language verges on the unintentionally comic.

from *Understanding Poetry*

COMMENTARY

Diction is the selection of words and phrases in speech and writing.

Dryden early used the word when criticizing Hobbes's remarks on Homer:

'Mr Hobbes, I say, begins the praise of Homer where he should have ended it. He tells us, that the first beauty of an Epic poem consists in diction, that is, in the choice of words and harmony of numbers; now, the words are the colouring of the work which in the order of nature is last to be considered.'

Dr Johnson said diction was 'a system of words . . . refined from the grossness of domestic use'. Lady Macbeth says she will use a knife to murder the King. A knife to Johnson was 'an instrument used by butchers and cooks' and the word should never have been used by her. 'Words too familiar, or too remote,' he says, 'defeat the purpose of a poet.'

Learn.

In 1880, Leslie Stephen said, 'The style in which a woman is called a nymph—and women generally are "the fair"—in which shepherds are conscious swains, and a poet invokes the muses and strikes a lyre, and breathes on a reed, and a nightingale singing becomes Philomel "pouring her throat", represents a fashion as worn out as hoops and wigs. By the time of Wordsworth it was a mere survival—a dead form remaining after its true function had entirely vanished.'

'A fashion as worn out as hoops and wigs' refers to poetic diction which was artificial, conventional, mannered and pompous.

T. S. Eliot demands that poetic diction should show:

An easy commerce of the old and the new,
The common word exact without vulgarity,
The formal word precise but not pedantic.

In the light of these remarks and your own reading of poetry discuss the following:

1. Only certain words or grammatical arrangements of words are suitable for poetry.

2. 'It is impossible to maintain that the diction of poetry should be simply that of common life.'

3. 'The poetical language of an age should be the current language heightened, to any degree heightened and unlike itself.'

Consult W. Nowottny, *The Language Poets Use.*

PRACTICAL CRITICISM

1. Select words from this passage to show the poet's diction.

> In every mart that stands on Britain's Isle,
> In every village less revealed to fame,
> Dwells there, in cottage known about a mile,
> A matron old, whom we school-mistress name,
> Who boasts unruly brats with birch to tame:
> They grieven sore in durance vile y-pent,
> Awed by the power of uncontrollèd dame;
> And oft-times, as vagaries idly bent,
> For hair unkempt, or task unconned are sorely shent.
>
> And all in sight does rise a birchen tree,
> Which Learning near her little dome did stow,
> Whilom a twig of small regard to see,
> Though now so wide its waving branches flow;
> And work the simple vassals mickle woe:
> For not a wind might curl the leaves, that blew,
> But their limbs shuddered, and their pulse beat low;
> And as they looked, they found their horror grew,
> And shaped it into rods, and tingled at the view.

Shenstone, The School-Mistress

Write a critical appreciation of the language and verse-form in which Tennyson tells his narrative.

So sigh'd the King,
Muttering and murmuring at his ear, 'Quick, quick!
I fear it is too late, and I shall die.'
But the other swiftly strode from ridge to ridge,
Clothed with his breath, and looking, as he walk'd,
Larger than human on the frozen hills.
He heard the deep behind him, and a cry
Before. His own thought drove him like a goad.
Dry clash'd his harness in the icy caves
And barren chasms, and all to left and right
The bare black cliff clang'd round him, as he based
His feet on juts of slippery crag that rang
Sharp-smitten with the dint of armed heels—
And on a sudden, lo! the level lake,
And the long glories of the winter moon.

                    Tennyson, *Morte d'Arthur*

3. Compare and contrast the diction of Lawrence and Hopkins in
   these poems.

They are beyond me, are fishes.
I stand at the pale of my being
And look beyond, and see
Fish, in the outerwards,
As one stands on a bank and looks in.

I have waited with a long rod
And suddenly pulled a gold-and-greenish, lucent fish from below,
And had him fly like a halo round my head,
Lunging in the air on the line.

Unhooked his gorping, water-horny mouth,
And seen his horror-tilted eye,
His red-gold, water-precious, mirror-flat bright eye;
And felt him beat in my hand, with his mucous, leaping life-throb

                    D. H. Lawrence, *Fish*

The darksome burn, horseback brown,
His rollrock highroad roaring down,
In coop and in comb the fleece of his foam
Flutes and low to the lake falls home.

A windpuff-bonnet of fáwn-fróth
Turns and twindles over the broth
Of a pool so pitchblack, féll-frówning,
It rounds and rounds Despair to drowning.

Degged with dew, dappled with dew
Are the groins of the braes that the brook treads through,
Wiry heathpacks, flitches of fern,
And the beadbonny ash that sits over the burn.

What would the world be, once bereft
Of wet and of wildness? Let them be left,
O let them be left, wildness and wet;
Long live the weeds and the wilderness yet.

Hopkins, *Inversnaid*

5. METAPHOR/SIMILE

PASSAGES: from Isaac Watts's version of *Psalm XC* and *The Embankment* by T. E. Hulme.
CRITICS: James Reeves and Babette Deutsch.

Among the chief resources of poetry are the devices we call metaphor and simile. Simile is the simpler to perceive and to understand; metaphor is the more compressed and suggestive. If you wish to explain to someone what something looks like which he has not seen before, you may do this by comparing it to something else. If you wish to extend the resources of language, you can do this by inventing metaphors. It is probable that in the earliest stages in the development of our language, this was the means by which much of the language itself was created. Our ancestors had something like our word 'stone' to denote the hard, mineral object we all know. When they wanted to convey the idea of someone or something remaining perfectly motionless, they coined the word 'to stand', which is connected with 'stone'. Originally, then, the verb 'to stand' (which to us is not metaphorical at all) meant 'to behave like a stone'—that is, 'to keep still'. Thus metaphor—seeing one thing in terms of another—is at the root of language, and poetry extends its range by the use of metaphor; metaphor itself is a sort of compressed simile. If you think of the idea of 'time', it is very difficult to convey it to anyone else. All we know is that it 'flows' or progresses from one moment to the next, one year to another. If we say that time flows, we imply that it moves in a fixed course, like a river. In the word 'flow' we imply a comparison with a river.

> Time like an ever-rolling stream
> Bears all its sons away;
> They fly forgotten as a dream
> Dies at the opening day.

So Isaac Watts, paraphrasing the Psalmist, describes the fleeting nature of human life, as distinct from the eternity of God. He uses two similes, one to suggest the relentless passage of time, the other

25

to suggest the impermanence of human life. When Shakespeare, in *Macbeth,* wanted to give a brief, vivid impression of the atmosphere of treachery and suspicion that existed in Scotland during the dictatorship of the usurper, he said, 'There's daggers in men's smiles.' He might have said, 'Beneath an appearance of cordiality men conceal treacherous intentions, as if they were concealing daggers beneath innocent-looking cloaks.' This is the full meaning of his words. But how much more compressed and graphic is the simple five-word sentence, 'There's daggers in men's smiles.'

from *Understanding Poetry*

T. E. Hulme wanted no decoration, no ornament. If he argued against plain speech, it was because he held that plain speech was inaccurate, that new metaphors, that fancy, make for precision. Witness even so slight a thing as 'the fantasia of a fallen gentleman on a cold, bitter night' entitled 'The Embankment':

> Once, in finesse of fiddles found I ecstasy,
> In the flash of gold heels on the hard pavement.
> Now see I
> That warmth's the very stuff of poesy.
> O, God, make small
> The old star-eaten blanket of the sky
> That I may fold it round me and in comfort lie.

Looked at closely, these lines might be taken as more than an example of Hulme's imagist theory of poetry, as, indeed, a metaphorical restatement of the changed demands of the art. The imagists wanted the warmth of true-tongued feeling; they wanted a sky that had been over-extended by 'poetic' usage to become once more something they could relate, 'star-eaten' and remote though it was, to the shivering human. They wanted words that would give the sting of experience, endured and known. Hence the emphasis on the concrete detail—the object seen, heard, smelled, tasted and touched, on the metaphor that has the force of a phys cal sensation. They agreed with Aristotle that for the poet 'the greatest thing by far is to have a command of metaphor. This alone cannot be imparted to another; it is the mark of genius, for to make good metaphors implies an eye for resemblances.'

from *Poetry in Our Time*

COMMENTARY

Babette Deutsch mentions Hulme's imagist theory of poetry. Hulme maintained that the chief aim of poetry was to achieve accurate description, and to prove that beauty might be found in small commonplace things. The Imagists used concentrated visual images 'hard and dry', often in free verse.

Consult P. F. Baum, *The Principles of English Versification.*

Metaphor (Greek *metaphorá*, transference; to carry over) is an explicit identification of essentially dissimilar things. We see in the metaphor the idea of similarity in dissimilarity. There's no poetry in identifying things that look alike. 'But far the greatest thing,' as Aristotle said, 'is a gift for metaphor. For this alone cannot be learnt from others and is a sign of inborn power.' Johnson recognized here 'a great excellence in style, when used with propriety, for it gives you two ideas for one.'

The metaphors in these lines are expressed as definite statements:

Life's but a walking shadow.

The moon was a ghostly galleon.

In

Tiger! Tiger! burning bright
In the forests of the night

the tiger is not a fire, but fire is implied. The poet therefore is using a compressed metaphor.

A mixed metaphor combines two metaphors incongruously, revealing a confusion of ideas:

I smell a rat in the air: I shall nip it in the bud.

A *simile* (Latin *similis,* like) makes a comparison for purposes of explanation, reference or ornament, introduced by a word such as *like, as, such* or *seems*. It can be brief:

I wandered lonely as a cloud
That floats on high o'er vales and hills.

Thy soul was like a star, and dwelt apart;
Thou hadst a voice whose sound was like the sea.

or sustained, known then as the epic simile. An example is the last two stanzas of *The Scholar Gipsy* by Matthew Arnold.

To say 'My heart is like a singing bird' is a simile, but to say that a girl looks like a duchess is not.

PRACTICAL CRITICISM

1. Comment on the following. Which of them are not similes? Which of them are decorative? Which of them has 'richness of suggestion'?

(*a*) That politician is like a fox.

(*b*) He wandered as if lost in a dream.

(*c*) A dingo is like a dog.

(*d*) As idle as a painted ship
Upon a painted ocean.

(*e*) Red as a rose is she.

(*f*) There is sweet music here that softer falls
Than petals from blown roses on the grass.

(*g*) The shadows now so long do grow,
That brambles like tall cedars show,
Mole-hills seem mountains, and the ant
Appears a monstrous elephant.

2. Make a critical examination of the use of metaphor and simile in the following passages. Are the metaphors ornaments only, or do they contain the 'sting of experience'?

(*a*)   She should have died hereafter;
There would have been a time for such a word.
To-morrow, and to-morrow, and to-morrow,
Creeps in this petty pace from day to day,
To the last syllable of recorded time;
And all our yesterdays have lighted fools
The way to dusty death. Out, out, brief candle!
Life's but a walking shadow, a poor player,
That struts and frets his hour upon the stage,
And then is heard no more; it is a tale
Told by an idiot, full of sound and fury,
Signifying nothing.

Shakespeare, *Macbeth*

[handwritten margin notes: Metaphors appreciate]

(b)   Hail to thee, blithe Spirit!
          Bird thou never wert,
       That from Heaven, or near it,
          Pourest thy full heart
    In profuse strains of unpremeditated art.

          Higher still and higher
             From the earth thou springest
          Like a cloud of fire;
             The blue deep thou wingest,
    And singing still dost soar, and soaring ever singest.

          In the golden lightning
             Of the sunken sun,
          O'er which clouds are bright'ning,
             Thou dost float and run,
    Like an unbodied joy whose race is just begun.

          The pale purple even
             Melts around thy flight;
          Like a star of Heaven
             In the broad daylight
    Thou art unseen, but yet I hear thy shrill delight.

          Keen as are the arrows
             Of that silver sphere,
          Whose intense lamp narrows
             In the white dawn clear,
    Until we hardly see—we feel that it is there.

                                   Shelley, *To a Skylark*

3. To what purpose do you think Arnold uses the epic simile
   below? What are the properties of this type of image? Compare
   with passage (a), referring to visual qualities.

       As some rich woman, on a winter's morn,
       Eyes through her silken curtains the poor drudge
       Who with numb blacken'd fingers makes her fire—
       At cock-crow, on a starlit winter's morn,
       When the frost flowers the whiten'd window-panes—
       And wonders how she lives, and what the thoughts

Of that poor drudge may be; so Rustum eyed
The unknown adventurous youth, who from afar
Came seeking Rustum, and defying forth
All the most valiant chiefs; long he perused
His spirited air, and wonder'd who he was.
For very young he seem'd, tenderly rear'd;
Like some young cypress, tall, and dark, and straight,
Which in a queen's secluded garden throws
Its slight dark shadow on the moonlit turf,
By midnight, to a bubbling fountain's sound—
So slender Sohrab seem'd, so softly rear'd.

Matthew Arnold, *Sohrab and Rustum*

6. IMAGERY

POEMS: H. W. Longfellow, from *A Psalm of Life*; Gerard Manley
Hopkins, from *The Wreck of the Deutschland*; Andrew Marvell,
from *To his Coy Mistress*.
CRITIC: H. Coombes.

We may consider whether Longfellow had his mind or his eyes on
his subject when he wrote his famous quatrain:

> Lives of great men all remind us
> We may make our lives sublime,
> And, departing, leave behind us
> Footprints on the sands of time.

It is probable that the image of the last two lines has been even
more instrumental than the sentiment expressed in the whole
verse, in making Longfellow a main contributor to autograph
albums. For it is a romantically vague 'mysterious' metaphor. It
is a very bad metaphor too. First, sands like these, in their extent
and lack of any forward movement, do not in themselves suggest
time: surely Longfellow has confusedly in mind the sands of the
hour-glass, which do really run, and he hazily and inappropriately
introduces footprints. And in any case, he is intending to suggest
leaving a lasting name behind, and what is more evanescent than
footprints in sand? Also, everybody, the good and the bad, leave
such footprints; they are not reserved as a privilege for those who
are inspired by the thoughts of the 'lives of great men'. The metaphor is no more than a gesture towards solemn impressiveness,
and is empty of sensible meaning. It has been popular because,
supported by words with an easy emotional appeal content, such
as 'sublime', 'departing', 'leave behind us', it has a vague seashore
mystery or Man Friday atmosphere about it. In a sensible reading
the last two lines are immediately felt as bathos. Whatever we
think of the sentiment expressed in the first two lines, the image
does nothing to support it; in fact, as we perceive the emptiness
of the image we are likely to pay the less attention to the sentiment
or thought. We are not likely to listen to the moral maxims of an
author when we discern such evidence of blurred thinking.

Arising from consideration of Longfellow's metaphor about sand, it is interesting to note certain images of Hopkins and of Marvell. In 'The Wreck of the *Deutschland*', Hopkins writes:

> I am soft sift
> In an hourglass—at the wall
> Fast, but mined with a motion, a drift,
> And it crowds and it combs to the fall . . .

This image, though difficult at first to grasp, will be found to succeed where Longfellow's fails: it is apt, precise and vivid. The process of the sand's sinking in the glass has been observed with delicate accuracy, and the perception is now brought imaginatively into play to present with sensitive exactness a mental-spiritual condition. The motion of the sand powerfully conveys the poet's feeling of an inner weakness and doubt, of a lack of solidity which is undermining him, of a fear of the hastening 'drift' towards failure and dissolution. The weakness is not obviously apparent but it is central and dangerous. Anyone who has stepped on moving sand will have had a frightening feeling of loss of effective action, and there is something of that feeling here. We may think too of the Bible house that was built on sand. The fourth line, the climax of the movement, suggests how inexorably the dissolution proceeds when there is no core of stability. Diction, sound, movement, are of course integral in this superb image, as they are in all richly suggestive images: the image makes us feel sensuously and physically, simultaneously with our grasping the 'intellectual' meaning.

The second image of which Longfellow's can remind us is from Marvell's 'To his Coy Mistress':

> But at my back I always hear
> Time's wingèd chariot hurrying near;
> And yonder all before us lie
> Deserts of vast eternity.

And this itself may recall another: set by the side of this Herrick's 'Gather ye rosebuds while ye may, Old Time is still a-flying', and Marvell's distinction will be immediately felt. The comparison is offered here, not just to establish Marvell's superiority, but to help demonstration. That superiority is in many directions, of which one is the fully realized image. Herrick gives a general and conventional image in conventional terms; Marvell is personally involved in a particular situation, which nevertheless is a representative one for all mankind, and this involvement, the situation being what it is, gives rise to the strong but controlled emotion of his lines. The contrast between the movement and hurry of the life in time, never pausing, and the motionless blank of eternity, is the substance of the vision which, expressed with the peculiar power of the poet's language, conveys this emotion. The vision has a grim quality: the poet is pursued ceaselessly by thoughts of the ever-nearing chariot whose wheels are always audible; there is no escape from the life and laws of time, there is no turning he can take. Ahead for him (and for everyone), is the stillness, the bareness, the sterility, the dullness of eternity. The onward movement of life carried compensations of splendour with it—the chariot is 'winged'; static eternity has none. And (paradoxically) the knowledge of those splendours makes his thought the more solemn, and his serious thought makes the splendours appear all the more attractive. Such an account of the material of the image appears clumsily abstract when compared with the poet's swift, 'concretizing' power. Marvell has given emotional significance to the conception of time and eternity, involving all mankind, in a particular, largely visual image. The visual element in the image is emotionally charged, it is inseparable from the moving thought (which the relentless rhythm is part of, too); in the same way, the predominantly tactual image 'sticking on his hands'* was seen to make a strong immediate impact and to have rich suggestiveness. (Though not actually relevant to a discussion mainly about imagery, the fruitful use of the word 'all' in Marvell's lines can be noted: it signifies that all the space before us is desert; that this blank eternity is all, there is nothing else; and it is there for all of us.)

from *Literature and Criticism*

COMMENTARY

Imagery (Latin *imago,* a likeness) is an integral part of a poem. It should never be mere decoration. An image may be, for example,

* 'Now does he feel
His secret murders sticking on his hands.'
Angus says this about Macbeth.

a visual image, a copy of a sensation. Most images producing a
mental picture are visual. But they can also suggest what is heard
(audible, auditory), smelt (olfactory), touched (tactile) or tasted
(gustatory). These sensory types of image are perhaps best
remembered as physical.

A poem may have a series of images which support or oppose
one another. Burns uses images in this stanza which enhance each
other by contrast:

> O my luve is like a red, red rose,
> That's newly sprung in June;
> O my luve is like the melodie,
> That's sweetly play'd in tune.

A particular image, or closely related images, may recur in a
poem or play so as to become dominant imagery. In Shakespeare's
plays we have the images of weeds and disease in *Hamlet*; of
cruelty and torture in *King Lear*; of blood and darkness in *Macbeth*;
of opulence and enjoyment in *Antony and Cleopatra*.

Many poets have individual images. Donne's poems have
images drawn from exploration, science, theology; Shelley has
images of clouds, stars, winds, the sea. Look for examples. Often
the image illustrates the poet's experience.

Another kind of imagery comes through association. Association is an essential part of allusion. Used by poets, allusion brings
a wide world of experience outside the limitations of plain statement—this imagery may be visual, emotional, a sense of history.

> What resounds
> In fable or romance of Uther's son
> Begirt with British and Armoric knights;
> And all who since, baptized or infidel
> Jousted in Aspramont or Montalban,
> Damasco, or Marocco, or Trebisond . . .

See Caroline Spurgeon, *Shakespeare's Imagery*;
    C. Day Lewis, *The Poetic Image*.

PRACTICAL CRITICISM

Consider the imagery of each of the following, bearing in mind
these points:

(i) What do you understand by the phrase 'realization of experience'? Refer closely to the critical passage above.

(ii) How far is the imagery of each extract indicative of sharpness and accuracy of observation?

(iii) How appropriate is the imagery to each poet's meaning and purpose?

(iv) How successfully does each image 'concretize' the experience which the poet is trying to communicate?

(a) And still she slept an azure-lidded sleep,
In blanched linen, smooth and lavender'd,
While he from forth the closet brought a heap
Of candied apple, quince, and plum, and gourd,
With jellies soother than the creamy curd.

(b) Poor naked wretches, whereso'er you are,
That bide the pelting of this pitiless storm,
How shall your houseless heads and unfed sides
Your loop'd and window'd raggedness, defend you
From seasons such as these? O, I have ta'en
Too little care of this. Take physic, pomp, . . .

(c) One gate there only was, and that looked East
On the other side; which, when the arch-felon saw,
Due entrance he disdained, and in contempt
At one slight bound high overleaped all bound
Of hill or highest wall, and sheer within
Lights on his feet.

(d) Some frolic drunkard, reeling from a feast,
Provokes a brawl, and stabs you for a jest.
Yet ev'n these heroes, mischievously gay,
Lords of the street, and terrors of the way,
Flush'd as they are with folly, youth and wine,
Their prudent insults to the poor confine.

(e) Yet is she curster than the bear by kind,
And harder-hearted than the aged oak,
More glib than oil, more fickle than the wind,
Stiffer than steel, no sooner bent but broke.

(*f*) Care-charming Sleep, thou easer of all woes,
    Brother to Death, sweetly thyself dispose
    On this afflicted prince: fall like a cloud,
    In gentle showers; give nothing that is loud,
    Or painful to his slumbers; easy, light,
    And as a purling stream, thou son of Night
    Pass by his troubled senses; sing his pain,
    Like hollow murmuring wind or silver rain;
    Into this prince gently, oh, gently glide,
    And kiss him into slumbers like a bride.

(*g*) Have you seen but a bright lily grow
        Before rude hands have touched it?
    Have you marked but the fall of the snow
        Before the soil hath smutched it?
    Have you felt the wool of beaver,
        Or swan's down ever?
    Or have smelt o' the bud o' the brier
        Or the nard in the fire?
        Or have tasted the bag of the bee?
    O so white, O so soft, O so sweet is she!

7. CACOPHONY/EUPHONY

POEM: *Popularity* by Robert Browning.
CRITIC: Lascelles Abercrombie.

Euphony at bottom is the adaptation of language to convenience of articulation. A sentence hard to pronounce is said to lack euphony; but it does not follow that it will be unpleasant hearing: we sympathize with the trouble of the speaker, or are conscious of our own. But, whether the result be pleasant or not, euphony may be deliberately violated in poetry, if something expressive is to be gained. Browning, for instance, often chose to force on us the expressive sound of his syllables by downright cacophony. His *Popularity* shows a masterly power of alternating euphony and cacophony exactly as the occasion requires. It is no glib sort of euphony which this stanza gives us, for example, but that rare euphony which can hold a wealth of sharply contrasted sounds in strong and intricate discipline:

> Who has not heard how Tyrian shells
>   Enclosed the blue, that dye of dyes,
> Whereof one drop worked miracles
>   And coloured like Astarte's eyes
> Raw silk the merchant sells?

But from that rich ceremonious flow of vowels and consonants Browning proceeds to this:

> Yet there's the dye—in that rough mesh
>   The sea has only just o'er-whisper'd!
> Live whelks, the lips'-beard dripping fresh
>   As if they still the water's lisp heard
> Through foam the rock-weeds thresh.

If not quite cacophony, that is certainly not euphony. The tongue has to walk delicately there, for fear of tripping among those jostling consonants and abrupt vowels. But the very absence of euphony compels us to notice how vigorously the sound of the words suggests the washing of sea-water. Instantly, however, the mood changes and expands, and at once an exquisite and most noticeable euphony surprises us with its contrast; now it is the inviting ease with which syllable follows syllable, that opens to us a subtler and less imitative propriety of sound to sense:

> Enough to furnish Solomon
>   Such hangings for his cedar-house,
> That, when gold-robed he took the throne
>   In that abyss of blue, the Spouse
> Might swear his presence shone

> Most like the centre-spike of gold
>   Which burns deep in the blue-bell's womb,
> What time, with ardours manifold,
>   The bee goes singing to her groom,
> Drunken and overbold.

And then, after that lordly music, how does the poem end? With a cacophony that many readers still, it appears, find decidedly shocking:

> And there's the extract, flasked and fine,
>   And priced and saleable at last!
> And Hobbs, Nobbs, Stokes and Nokes combine
>   To paint the future from the past
> Put blue into their line.

> Hobbs hints blue,—straight he turtle eats:
>   Nobbs prints blue,—claret crowns his cup:
> Nokes outdares Stokes in azure feats,—
>   Both gorge. Who fished the murex up?
> What porridge had John Keats?

What makes the words so remarkably animated here? It is the intensity of ferocious and amused contempt with which they are charged. And where do we find that? Scarcely at all in their meaning, almost entirely in their sound.

from *The Theory of Poetry*

COMMENTARY

Euphony (Greek *euphōnia*, sweetness of sound). Pleasing sound, as in Milton's

> In shadier bower
> More sacred and sequestered, though but feigned
> Pan or Silvanus never slept, nor Nymph
> Nor Faunus haunted.

Cacophony (Greek *kakos*, bad, *phōnē*, sound). Ugly sound, which may not always be deliberate. Here Browning uses it with effect:

> Imagine the whole, then execute the parts—fancy the fabric
> Quite, ere you build, ere steel strike fire from quartz,
>   Ere mortar dab brick.

Onomatopoeia (Greek from *ónoma*, name, and *poieîn*, to make). The formation of words from sounds which seem to suggest and reinforce the meaning. This accounts for words like *murmur, cuckoo, sizzle, twitter*. When the sound is made 'an echo to the sense', onomatopoeia has a real value. So many English words are onomatopoeic that the poet choosing the right word for meaning will find it fits often for sound also. Clear speaking will bring out the fullness of the sound. Here are examples from Tennyson:

> I chatter over stony ways
> In little sharps and trebles,
> I bubble into eddying bays,
> I babble on the pebbles.

and Kipling:

> And the fenders grind and heave,
> And the derricks clack and grate, as the tackle hooks the crate,
> And the fall-rope whines through the sheave . . .

Alliteration (as if from Latin *ad literam*, according to the letter). This device, sometimes called head rhyme or initial rhyme, is the close repetition, not of the same letter, but of the same sound, usually at the beginning of words.

> All the blue bonnets are bound for the Border.

> The sad, sea-sounding wastes of Lyonesse.

Assonance. Where the stressed vowels in the words agree but not the consonants, as in *fate, take.*

Consonance. Identical consonant-sounds in the words and differing vowel-sounds, as in *stain, stone.*

PRACTICAL CRITICISM

1. In *The Prelude* Wordsworth tells us of the time when first his mind

> With conscious pleasure opened to the charm
> Of words in tuneful order, found them sweet
> For their own *sakes,* a passion and a power.

Discuss the significance of what Wordsworth says here, and illustrate how the particular sounds of words have their own particular effects in poetry.

2. Comment on the sounds used in the extracts below, and on how the poet has employed them to reflect his meaning.

(*a*) (describing the cranes)
> Cranking their jarring melancholy cry
> Through the long journey of the cheerless sky.

(*b*) Without a motion, save of their big hearts
> Heaving in pain, and horribly convulsed
> With sanguine feverous boiling gurge of pulse.

(*c*) But when loud surges lash the sounding shore,
> The hoarse, rough verse should like the torrent roar.
> When Ajax strives, some rock's vast weight to throw,
> The line too labours, and the words move slow;
> Not so, when swift Camilla scours the plain,
> Flies o'er the unbending corn, and skims along the main.

3. Write an appraisal of the following poem, paying special attention to theme and development, verse-form, rhythm and rhyme.

> Sweet Day, so cool, so calm, so bright,
> The bridal of the earth and sky,
> The dew shall weep thy fall to-night;
>   For thou must die.

Sweet Rose, whose hue angry and brave
Bids the rash gazer wipe his eye,
Thy root is ever in its grave,
                    And thou must die.

Sweet Spring, full of sweet days and roses,
A box where sweets compacted lie,
My Music shows ye have your closes,
                    And all must die.

Only a sweet and virtuous soul,
Like season'd timber, never gives;
But though the whole world turn to coal,
                    Then chiefly lives.

                    George Herbert, *Virtue*

8. CONNECTION THROUGH IMAGERY

POEM: *To Autumn* by John Keats.
CRITIC: Reuben Arthur Brower.

Season of mists and mellow fruitfulness,
　　Close bosom-friend of the maturing sun;
Conspiring with him how to load and bless
　　With fruit the vines that round the thatch-eves run;
To bend with apples the moss'd cottage-trees,
　　And fill all fruit with ripeness to the core;
　　　　To swell the gourd, and plump the hazel shells
　　With a sweet kernel; to set budding more,
And still more, later flowers for the bees,
Until they think warm days will never cease,
　　For summer has o'er-brimm'd their clammy cells.

Who hath not seen thee oft amid thy store?
　　Sometimes whoever seeks abroad may find
Thee sitting careless on a granary floor,
　　Thy hair soft-lifted by the winnowing wind;
Or on a half-reap'd furrow sound asleep,
　　Drows'd with the fume of poppies, while thy hook
　　　　Spares the next swath and all its twined flowers;
And sometimes like a gleaner thou dost keep
　　Steady thy laden head across a brook;
　　Or by a cyder-press, with patient look,
　　　　Thou watchest the last oozings hours by hours.

Where are the songs of Spring? Ay, where are they?
　　Think not of them, thou hast thy music too,—
While barred clouds bloom the soft-dying day,
　　And touch the stubble-plains with rosy hue;
Then in a wailful choir the small gnats mourn
　　Among the river sallows, borne aloft
　　　　Or sinking as the light wind lives or dies;
And full-grown lambs loud bleat from hilly bourn;

Hedge-crickets sing; and now with treble soft
The red-breast whistles from a garden-croft;
And gathering swallows twitter in the skies.

Study of the imagery of Keats's ode will show how a succession
of images, becoming something more than mere succession, im-
perceptibly blends into metaphor. We shall also discover how
groups of images are linked and how imagery works as design.
(The method of analysis used is a good example of tracing continuities.) We may begin by merely noting what Keats gives in the
way of images. In the first stanza: we have 'to load and bless',
'round the thatch-eves run', 'to bend', '(to) fill . . . the core', 'to
swell the gourd', '(to) plump the hazel shells', 'to set budding' and
'o'er-brimm'd their clammy cells'. As in his other odes Keats
tends to group together images from a single sense; here almost
all are tactile-muscular, though there is no good name for the
weighing, cupping sensations which fell distinctly in hand and
lips as we read these expressions. Because the sensations are closely
related, almost any one image draws in the rest by attraction. 'To
fill' becomes also 'to round' and 'to load'; and even words that
properly should not have such meanings absorb them. So 'round'
in 'round the thatch-eves run' trembles on the brink of meanings
with which it has no logical connection. Together all the images
of the stanza give rise to an over-meaning, a tactile awareness of
fruitioning. In this evocation of a common, though hardly name-
able meaning we have the first step from succession of images to
metaphor.

The over-meaning in the first stanza of the ode leads insensibly
to the central metaphor of the poem, the figure of Autumn. Since
we have already lived its powers in our senses, we quite easily
accept Autumn as person and divinity. We have also been prepared by the direct address in the opening lines of the poem and
by the expressions joining Autumn with the sun, the natural
object we most readily deify. Keats has made us feel that they are
in the closest possible relationship, that they work together,
almost breathe together as a single life-force: in the slow-paced
rhythm of the ode we realize the full etymological force of
'conspiring'.

The being so unobtrusively and yet so warmly realized appears
in a series of exquisite plastic poses. The images are now mainly
visual; they are most often glimpses of arrested movement. Where

there is motion, as in 'the winnowing wind', it is a kind of motion-in-repose, the hair remains 'soft-lifted' as in sculpture. Surely nothing could be nearer complete rest than 'the last oozings hours by hours'. The single image from another sense comes with a slight though muted shock:

> Drows'd with the fume of poppies,

but here too the final effect is of slow motion to sleep. The Autumn metaphor as a whole conveys the sense of tremendous leisure, the great pause, the slowing down of autumnal life.

There is again a slight jar in the shift to another area of sensation:

> Where are the songs of Spring? Ay, where are they?

Against images that recall the mellow richness and the repose of the preceding stanzas (so Keats alludes to what he has been saying), the sounds of autumn arise. They have a peculiar character, which accounts in part for their metaphorical power. Look closely at the language of the autumnal sound images: 'in a wailful choir the *small* gnats *mourn*', 'aloft or *sinking*', '*light* wind lives or *dies*', 'loud bleat *from hilly bourn*', '*hedge*-crickets sing', 'treble *soft* . . . whistles *from a garden-croft*', '*gathering* swallows *twitter in the skies*'. The italics indicate the curious way in which the sounds are qualified. They are to be felt as withdrawing, diminished things. They are soft, mournful, small or undulating and uncertain (the point of 'aloft or sinking' as coloured by 'lives or dies'); or they come from a distance, or they are connected with confined places and with shutting in. This is the linking that counts most as metaphor in the last phase of the poem. To the autumn richness and slowing down Keats adds a sense of closing in and withdrawal, a poignant autumnal note. Such, very roughly outlined, are the attitudes Keats conveys through his images and especially through the metaphorical patterns in which they merge.

In our reading of Keats's ode we have begun to see how connection through imagery is made. The behaviour of these images, the way in which they compose metaphors is typical. We note, for example, that the images in the opening stanza of the poem give rise to an over-meaning, a special sense of fruitioning. In the last stanza a similar meaning, one of diminution and withdrawal, grows out of the sound images. These groupings are potent not merely as sets of observed facts, of actual autumn phenomena—

which we suppose they are. . . . Though we connect the images in Keats's lines through simple analogies of time and space, we also link them by another sort of analogy, the analogy of sensation. If we respond to Keats's words at all, we must be conscious of qualitative likeness in each of the sense experiences they evoke. Our consciousness of similarity is qualitative in the primitive physiological meaning of the term; it consists, for instance, in felt similarities of muscular tension or release. And we must pass through these special qualifications of sensation if we are to reach the over-meaning. Keats, and all poets who compose at this level of intensity, connect images for us by this special type of analogy while also expressing other simpler likenesses. They create those fuller alliances of analogy which are the surest sign of imaginative power.

from *The Fields of Light*

PRACTICAL CRITICISM

1. R. A. Brower also says of *To Autumn*, this 'may be regarded as the poem that the eighteenth-century describers were trying to write'. How do these lines on spring flowers by James Thomson an eighteenth-century poet, differ from Keats's poem?

> Along the blushing Borders, bright with Dew,
> And in yon mingled Wilderness of Flowers,
> Fair-handed Spring unbosoms every Grace:
> Throws out the Snow-drop, and the Crocus first;
> The Daisy, Primrose, Violet darkly blue,
> And Polyanthus of unnumber'd Dyes;
> The yellow Wall-Flower, stain'd with iron Brown;
> And lavish Stock that scents the Garden round:
> From the soft Wing of vernal Breezes shed,
> Anemonies: Auriculas, enrich'd
> With shining Meal o'er all their velvet Leaves;
> And full Renunculas, of glowing Red.

2. Dr Johnson said, 'Talking of conversation, there must, in the first place, be knowledge, there must be materials; in the second place there must be command of words; in the third place there must be imagination, to place things in such views as they are not commonly seen in; and in the fourth place there must be

presence of mind and resolution that is not to be overcome by failures.'

How much of this do you think applies to writing poetry?

3. Write an appreciation of the following poem, considering in particular these aspects of the imagery:

(i) What type of pictures had the poet in mind?

(ii) Do you feel any 'consciousness of similarity' between the images? Discuss this phrase in the light of R. A. Brower's analysis of *To Autumn*.

(iii) Are you able to trace any 'continuity of imagery'? First of all define carefully how you understand that phrase.

(iv) Discuss the images in relation to Brower's concept of 'over-meaning'. Define this term carefully, and illustrate with quotations from Keats's Odes.

No, no, go not to Lethe, neither twist
   Wolf's-bane, tight-rooted, for its poisonous wine;
Nor suffer thy pale forehead to be kiss'd
   By nightshade, ruby grape of Proserpine;
Make not your rosary of yew-berries,
   Nor let the beetle, nor the death-moth be
      Your mournful Psyche, nor the downy owl
A partner in your sorrow's mysteries;
   For shade to shade will come too drowsily,
      And drown the wakeful anguish of the soul.

But when the melancholy fit shall fall
   Sudden from heaven like a weeping cloud,
That fosters the droop-headed flowers all,
   And hides the green hill in an April shroud;
Then glut thy sorrow on a morning rose,
   Or on the rainbow of the salt sand-wave,
      Or on the wealth of globèd peonies;
Or if thy mistress some rich anger shows,
   Emprison her soft hand, and let her rave,
      And feed deep, deep upon her peerless eyes.

She dwells with Beauty—Beauty that must die;
And Joy, whose hand is ever at his lips
Bidding adieu; and aching Pleasure nigh,
   Turning to poison while the bee-mouth sips:
Ay, in the very temple of Delight
    Veil'd Melancholy has her sovran shrine,
      Though seen of none save him whose strenuous tongue
Can burst Joy's grape against his palate fine;
   His soul shall taste the sadness of her might;
    And be among her cloudy trophies hung.

Keats, *Ode on Melancholy*

9. GENERALIZATION/CONCRETE PARTICULARITY

PASSAGES: Shakespeare, from *Richard II* and *Troilus and Cressida*.
CRITIC: L. C. Knights.

No account of the development of Shakespeare's blank verse in general terms can be very satisfactory. A comparison will help to point my few necessary generalizations. Richard's lament at Pomfret is a fairly typical example of the early set speeches:

> And here have I the daintiness of ear
> To check time broke in a disorder'd string;
> But, for the concord of my state and time,
> Had not an ear to hear my true time broke.
> I wasted time, and now doth time waste me;
> For now hath time made me his numbering clock:
> My thoughts are minutes; and with sighs they jar
> Their watches on unto mine eyes, the outward watch,
> Whereto my finger, like a dial's point,
> Is pointing still, in cleansing them from tears.
> Now, sir, the sound that tells what hour it is
> Are clamorous groans, which strike upon my heart,
> Which is the bell: so sighs and tears and groans
> Show minutes, times, and hours: but my time
> Runs posting on in Bolingbroke's proud joy,
> While I stand fooling here, his Jack o' the clock.

The only line that could possibly be mistaken for an extract from a later play is the last, in which the concentrated bitterness ('Jack o' the clock' has a wide range of relevant associations, and the tone introduces a significant variation in the rhythm) serves to emphasize the previous diffuseness. It is not merely that the imagery is elaborated out of all proportion to any complexity of thought or feeling, the emotion is suspended whilst the conceit is developed, as it were, in its own right. Similarly the sound and movement of the verse, the alliteration, repetition and

48

assonance, seem to exist as objects of attention in themselves rather than as the medium of a compulsive force working from within. Such emotion as is communicated is both vague and remote.

Set beside this the well-known speech of Ulysses:

> Time hath, my lord, a wallet at his back,
> Wherein he puts alms for oblivion,
> A great-siz'd monster of ingratitudes;
> Those scraps are good deeds past, which are devour'd
> As fast as they are made, forgot as soon
> As done. Perseverance, dear my lord,
> Keeps honour bright. To have done is to hang
> Quite out of fashion, like a rusty mail
> In monumental mockery. Take the instant way;
> For honour travels in a strait so narrow
> Where one but goes abreast. Keep then the path,
> For emulation hath a thousand sons
> That one by one pursue; if you give way,
> Or hedge aside from the direct forthright,
> Like to an enter'd tide they all rush by
> And leave you hindmost.

The verse of course is much more free, and the underlying speech movement gives a far greater range of rhythmic subtlety. The sound is more closely linked with—is, in fact, an intimate part of—the meaning. The imagery changes more swiftly. But these factors are only important as contributing to a major development: the main difference lies in the greater immediacy and concreteness of the verse. In reading the second passage more of the mind is involved, and it is involved in more ways. It does not contemplate a general emotion, it *lives* a particular experience. Crudely, the reader is not told that there is a constant need for action, he experiences a particular urgency.

This account could be substantiated in detail, but for my purpose it may be sufficient to point to a few of the means by which the reader is influenced in this way. Oblivion, at first a kind of negative presence, becomes (via 'monster') an active, devouring force, following hard on the heels of time. ('Forgot', balancing 'devoured', keeps the image in a proper degree of subordination.)

The perseverance which keeps honour bright introduces a sense of effort, as in polishing metal, and (after a particularly effective jibe at inactivity) the effort is felt as motion. Moreover, 'Take the instant way' and 'Keep then the path', involving muscular tension, suggest the strain of keeping foremost. In the next two lines the roar and clatter of emulation's thousand sons are audible, and immediately we feel the pressure of pursuit ('hedge aside' is no dead metaphor) and—in the movement of the verse, as though a dam had broken—the overwhelming tide of pursuers. The short and exhausted line, 'And leave you hindmost', is the lull after the wave has passed.

This line of development (continued in the plays of complete maturity) is central. Primarily it is a matter of technique—the words have a higher potency, they release and control a far more complex response than in the earlier plays—but it is much more than that. The kind of immediacy that I have indicated allows the greatest subtlety in particular presentment. (The thing 'which shackles accidents, and bolts up change' is *not* the same as 'The deed which puts an end to human vicissitude'), whilst 'the quick flow and the rapid change of the images', as Coleridge noted, require a 'perpetual activity of attention on the part of the reader', generate, we may say, a form of activity in which thought and feeling are fused in a new mode of apprehension. That is, the technical development implies—is dependent on—the development and unification of sensibility.

from *Scrutiny,* Vol. III

COMMENTARY

L. C. Knights contrasts the two Shakespearean passages above, and says 'the main difference lies in the greater immediacy and concreteness of the verse' in the speech of Ulysses.

'Immediacy' here means having actual contact, direct relation.

Concreteness of verse suggests the immediate experience of realities. It can be reached by close, precise description.

> Ay, but to die, and go we know not where;
> To lie in cold obstruction, and to rot;
> This sensible warm motion to become
> A kneaded clod . . .

PRACTICAL CRITICISM

1. What other qualities does Knights discover in the passage from
   Troilus and Cressida which makes it so effective in contrast with
   the passage from *Richard II*?

2. Bearing these qualities in mind, discuss the dramatic effective-
   ness of the following:

   (*a*)   Ecstasy!
       My pulse as yours doth temperately keep time,
       And makes as healthful music—it is not madness
       That I have uttered, bring me to the test
       And I the matter will re-word, which madness
       Would gambol from. Mother, for love of grace,
       Lay not that flattering unction to your soul,
       That not your trespass but my madness speaks,
       It will but skin and film the ulcerous place,
       Whiles rank corruption mining all within
       Infects unseen.

   (*b*) That hand which had the strength, even at your door,
       To cudgel you and make you take the hatch,
       To dive like buckets in concealed wells,
       To crouch in litter of your stable planks,
       To lie like pawns lock'd up in chests and trunks,
       To hug with swine, to seek sweet safety out
       In vaults and prisons, and to thrill and shake
       Even at the crying of your nation's crow,
       Thinking his voice an armed Englishman;
       Shall that victorious hand be feebled here,
       That in your chambers gave you chastisement?

   (*c*)   Here's a stay,
       That shakes the rotten carcase of old Death
       Out of his rags! Here's a large mouth, indeed,
       That spits forth death and mountains, rocks and seas,
       Talks as familiarly of roaring lions
       As maids of thirteen do of puppy-dogs.
       What cannoneer begot this lusty blood?
       He speaks plain cannon fire, and smoke and bounce:

He gives the bastinado with his tongue;
Our ears are cudgell'd; not a word of his
But buffets better than a fist of France.
'Zounds! I was never so bethump'd with words
Since I first call'd my brother's father dad.

3. Compare and contrast the two following passages, pointing out
whatever seems to you to be authentically Shakespearean.

(a) Hail, sovereign queen of secrets, who hast power
To call the fiercest tyrant from his rage,
And weep unto a girl; that hast the might
Even with an eye-glance, to choke Mars's drum
And turn th'alarm to whispers; that canst make
A cripple flourish with his crutch, and cure him
Before Apollo; that mayst force the king
To be his subject's vassal, and induce
Stale gravity to dance; the polled bachelor—
Whose youth, like wanton boys through bonfires,
Have skipped thy flame—at seventy thou canst catch
And make him, to the scorn of his hoarse throat,
Abuse young lays of love; what godlike power
Hast thou not power upon?

(b) All tongues speak of him, and the bleared sights
Are spectacled to see him: your prattling nurse
Into a rapture lets her baby cry
While she chats him: the kitchen malkin pins
Her richest lockram 'bout her reechy neck,
Clambering the walls to eye him: stalls, bulks, windows,
Are smother'd up, leads fill'd and ridges horsed
With variable complexions, all agreeing
In earnestness to see him: our veil'd dames
Commit the war of white and damask in
Their nicely-gawded cheeks to the wanton spoil
Of Phoebus' burning kisses: such a pother,
As if that whatsoever god who leads him
Were slily crept into his human powers,
And gave him graceful posture.

10. CONSISTENCY OF IMPRESSION

POEM: from *Hyperion* by John Keats
CRITIC: C. Day Lewis.

We should agree that images, be they never so surprising at first sight, should finally leave the reader with the impression that they are the natural language of their theme. But this does not imply they will have come easily, or naturally, to the poet. Keats's corrections on the opening lines of *Hyperion* are very much to the point here: and, though they have become a *locus classicus* of criticism, they will bear examination once again. Here is the final version:

> 1 Deep in the shady sadness of a vale
> Far-sunken from the healthy breath of morn,
> Far from the fiery noon, and eve's one star,
> Sat grey-hair'd Saturn, quiet as a stone,
> 5 Still as the silence round about his lair;
> Forest on forest hung about his head
> Like cloud on cloud. No stir of air was there,
> Not so much life as on a summer's day
> Robs not one light seed from the feather'd grass,
> 10 But where the dead leaf fell, there did it rest.

His first shot at lines 8–9 was,

> Not so much life as a young vulture's wing
> Would spread upon a field of green-ear'd corn:

What gave him the vulture was, possibly, the aerial view of Saturn suggested by 'Forest on forest hung about his head *Like cloud on cloud*', together with the suggestion of something dying—the immobility of the dying god, and a bird of prey circling above, waiting for the end. Then, I think, it occurred to Keats quite simply that there was an inconsistency between the idea of the vulture and that of 'a field of green-ear'd corn'; a vulture should be circling over a desert: besides, Saturn was a god, and his

dignity would be impaired by the association with so squalid a
bird: so line 8 was altered to 'Not so much life as what an eagle's
wing'. A more appropriate, god-like bird is introduced, the eagle
sacred to Saturn's usurper; and it may be also that Keats had
vaguely in mind the image which was shortly to appear in the
lines, cancelled later,

> Thus the old Eagle, drowsy with great grief,
> Sat moulting his weak Plumage never more
> To be restored or soar against the Sun.

But Keats was not satisfied. We can imagine him standing back
from the picture, asking himself what was wrong with it. And his
eye would pause upon the 'field of green-ear'd corn'. What is that
field doing here in a picture which represents age, stillness,
melancholy, impotence? So this incongruous symbol of youth
and fertility was painted out; and in its place comes

> Not so much life as on a summer's day
> Robs not at all the dandelion's fleece.

At last, consistency of impression had been reached: the dandelion,
a fitting association with a god who had gone to seed. 'Gone to
seed'; seedless, without posterity, a god without a future. And so
came the final version, tightening up the tension of the whole
passage, emphasizing the lifelessness of the scene with the delaying
stresses on the first five words of the second line,

> Not so much life as on a summer's day
>
> Robs not one light seed from the feather'd grass.

What we have seen there is a poet going all out for intensity of
expression; sacrificing certain points for it, and in the result
achieving also consistency of impression. The alterations to the
first draft reveal how conscious was the process: we can follow
the stages by which the poet, penetrating ever more deeply into
the meaning of his intuition, has at once been guided by it and
directed it, as a sculptor may be guided by the grain and contour
of the rudimentary block from which he is extracting a finished
form.

from *The Poetic Image*

PRACTICAL CRITICISM

Michelangelo said, 'What one takes most pains to do, should look as if it had been thrown off quickly, almost without effort—nay, despite the truth, as if it had cost no trouble. Take infinite pains to make something that looks effortless.'

Comment upon the improvements made by revision in the second version of each of the passages below:

(i)   Since then at an uncertain hour,
            Now ofttimes and now fewer,
        That anguish comes and makes me tell
            My ghastly aventure.

(ii)   Since then at an uncertain hour
            That agony returns:
        And till my ghastly tale is told,
            My heart within me burns.

Coleridge, *Ancient Mariner*

(i)   There is a dale in Ida, lovelier
        Than any in old Ionia, beautiful
        With emerald slopes of sunny sward, that lean
        Above the loud glenriver, which hath worn
        A path thro' steepdown granite walls below
        Mantled with flowering tendril twine. In front
        The cedarshadowy valleys open wide.
        Far-seen, high over all the God-built wall
        And many a snowycolumned range divine,
        Mounted with awful sculptures,—men and Gods,
        The work of Gods—bright on the dark-blue sky
        The windy citadel of Ilion
        Shone, like the crown of Troas. Hither came
        Mournful Œnone wandering forlorn
        Of Paris, once her playmate.

(ii)   There lies a vale in Ida, lovelier
        Than all the valleys of Ionian hills.
        The swimming vapour slopes across the glen,
        Puts forth an arm, and creeps from pine to pine,
        And loiters, slowly drawn. On either hand

The lawns and meadow-ledges midway down
Hang rich in flowers, and far below them roars
The long brook falling through the clov'n ravine
In cataract after cataract to the sea.
Behind the valley topmost Gargarus
Stands up and takes the morning: but in front
The gorges, opening wide apart, reveal
Troas and Ilion's column'd citadel,
The crown of Troas.

                     Hither came at noon
Mournful Œnone, wandering forlorn
Of Paris, once her playmate on the hills.

                               Tennyson, *Œnone*

11. POETIC THOUGHT

POEM: *A Poison Tree* by William Blake.
CRITIC: H. Coombes.

> I was angry with my friend:
> I told my wrath, my wrath did end.
> I was angry with my foe:
> I told it not, my wrath did grow.
>
> And I water'd it in fears,
> Night and morning with my tears;
> And I sunnèd it with smiles,
> And with soft deceitful wiles.
>
> And it grew both day and night,
> Till it bore an apple bright,
> And my foe beheld it shine
> And he knew that it was mine,
>
> And into my garden stole
> When the night had veil'd the pole:
> In the morning glad I see
> My foe outstretch'd beneath the tree.

The prose-meaning of the poem, the prose-thought, could be extracted to run something like this: 'As soon as I told my friend that I was angry with him, the anger died away; but when I was angry with my foe, I cherished the anger, and by cunning and deceitful behaviour I laid a trap for him which was his undoing.' This is what a simple summary would be like; and the extent of its inadequacy, despite its significance as a psychological 'truth,' to suggest the range and depth of experience that the poem covers, is some evidence of the presence of extraordinary poetic thought. Blake is concerned to express certain psychological facts: the release from an emotion or an attitude—anger here—that takes place when such an emotion or attitude is given utterance and comes into the open; the change from anger, when it is hidden, into the evil of dissimulation; the 'sweetness' and evil of revenge. But the facts are given a strange and complex potency, quite beyond what their value as 'true' facts can give, by the manner of their presentment.

The manner is that of a vision described with great clarity and definiteness. The poet is giving clear and vivid utterance to most subtle and ambiguous feelings; and it is the union of clearness of vision and complete simplicity of language with the profound ambiguity of his attitude that gives the poem its power. The poet is both good and evil: he is good and wise to speak openly to his friend, he is evil to use his wisdom, which degenerates into cunning, to overcome his foe. He is clear-headed and deliberate, but there is perhaps a touch of remorse, though no relenting, in his 'fears'; and his 'tears' are real as well as assumed. The 'smiles' and the 'soft deceitful wiles', noted down as evil, are at the same time felt to be delightful, and the sinister apple is a beautiful thing. The ambiguity continues to the end where the poet is 'glad' at the murderous victory he has won. A further ambiguity is felt in our recognition of the 'honest' confession of dishonest behaviour. Nearly all the poem is concerned with the development of the metaphor out of the word 'grow'; after the first verse of six short statements, and springing spontaneously out of it like natural growth, there is a marvellously easy and sure transition to the vividly concrete setting and action, out of which we can *extract* the prose-meaning, but *in* and *through* which we feel the wealth of the poet's *experience,* experience understood and controlled with such certainty as to be felt inevitably and profoundly true.

Consider the way in which the statements and the narrative work. In a poem of sixteen lines there are some sixteen clauses (not one to each line, however), and nearly every line is in a sense self-contained, yet so perfectly does the action 'grow' out of the initial terse but easily natural 'logic' that the poem is a most forcefully coherent whole. There is no feeling of thoughts having been clothed picturesquely; the vision, which is one of action, moves directly, the thought is fused in it. And it moves, not just by its intrinsic quality as vision, but by the inevitability and suggestiveness imparted by the poet's language: vision and language are one. The repetition of 'And' gives deliberateness and relentlessness, and this impression is enhanced by the quiet, even movement maintained throughout, the climax coming with the greater force for its being calm. But though the movement is quiet, it is emphatic; the speech-rhythm is heightened in such a way as to stress unostentatiously the key words, and analysis would show the rhymes to be magnificently used: it is unnecessary to demonstrate here a point that is so clear, but we may briefly note how the stresses in the first verse fall in the main on 'angry', 'friend', 'told', 'end', 'angry', 'foe', 'not', 'grow'; the verse movement and the sound work with this kind of unforced emphasis throughout.

The pattern of the poem is regular, but its regularity is functional; that is to say, the pattern makes for the clarity, the certainty, the coherence of the poetic statement. It seems the only possible expression for the ordering of the experience that led to the poetry. Through the low tones of the beginning of the stratagem and the insinuating sibilant sounds associated with his smiles and soft deceits, the temptation to gloat is felt to be growing, but it is never allowed to get out of hand; and after the shining apple has been seen by the foe (who is also an intending deceiver), the stealth of his action is suggested in the quiet falling quality of the words that describe it. The climax gains its great force by its being the culmination of an evil and inevitable-seeming process, by its quiet certainty and by the juxtaposition of 'glad' with the 'foe outstretch'd beneath the tree', where the poet's acceptance, uneager but assured, shocks despite his having led us with such certainty to such a culmination. The horror of his exultation is the greater for its being controlled. The word 'outstretch'd' contributes powerfully: it is a 'physical' word, its sound, even its appearance, emphasizing its meaning; and not only is it the more impressive for appearing against the glad and gladdening morning ('glad' can go with both 'morning' and 'I'), where, this being the time of the sun's rising and of birds' singing and of other manifestations of brightening life, its presence suggests more horror and 'ambiguity'; but it is also in strong meaning- and sound-contrast with 'stole': 'stole' . . . 'outstretch'd'—the stealthy act, the retribution; the word may also suggest 'outdone'.

Comprehensive analysis of the poem would reveal further implications: the significance of the conjunction and opposition of day and night, for example, and the mystery of darkness; the suggestion of Satan in the Garden of Eden, and the apple of the tree of knowledge. The poem provides a superb example of poetic thought: the experience of the duplicity of human behaviour is given concrete embodiment—the apple shines there for all of us—in the simple-complex action centring round the Poison Tree. It is a visionary, not a mystical poem; for though at some points we may not be sure of the precise prose-meaning (for instance, has 'veil'd the pole' a significance beyond its mysterious suggestiveness? Is the pole or pole-star emblematic of guide, conscience?), fundamentally we feel the profound 'meaning' of the vision, which is not oddly personal but has a universal human application. And we feel it not because of Blake's penetrating psychological faculty—though that is of course here in the poem—but because of his power to express his experience in words that are strong and vivid.

from *Literature and Criticism*

COMMENTARY

The critic is making a very important comment above when he says, 'it is the union of clearness of vision and complete simplicity of language with the profound ambiguity of his attitude that gives the poem its power.' We must consider the word 'ambiguity' because in poetry it has an extended sense. It implies double meaning, or an expression capable of more than one meaning.

William Empson has analysed seven types of ambiguity, and of these it is a great help to know the following: when 'a detail is effective in several ways at once'; when 'two or more alternative meanings are fully resolved into one'; when 'two apparently unconnected meanings are given simultaneously'; when 'the alternative meanings combine to make clear a complicated state of mind in the author'.

Empson shows in Shakespeare's line

Bare ruined choirs, where late the sweet birds sang

the various ways in which wintry trees resemble 'bare ruined choirs'—because they are places in which to sing, because they involve sitting in a row, are made of wood, are carved into knots, are part of a forest as monastery choirs are of a building.

By this enrichment and heightening of effect ambiguity is another essential resource of poetry.

'The apple of the tree of knowledge' in the critical passage above is symbolism (Greek *sumbállein*, to throw together), the drawing together of two different worlds. The apple of the tree of knowledge, in the words 'apple' and 'tree', denotes physical, limited things, but also stands for the temptation and the fall of man. Symbolism, therefore, stands for and reveals something else; the cross is a symbol of Christianity, the rose is a symbol of beauty, salt, as incorruptible, has been called the symbol of friendship.

A symbol in poetry differs from a symbol in mathematics, for there it is a sign for something definite. In poetry a symbol has many meanings and feelings which together reveal something often indefinite and inexpressible. The quality of a symbol, therefore, is not an exact resemblance of the concrete object named, but a version of another world with large and often profound suggestiveness.

Consult C. M. Bowra, *The Heritage of Symbolism*;
Edmund Wilson, *Axel's Castle*, Chapter 1.

PRACTICAL CRITICISM

1. Consider the style (diction, imagery, sound effects) and treatment of subject-matter in each of the following:

(*a*) *Twa Corbies*

As I was walking all alane,
I heard twa corbies making a mane;
And t'ane unto the tither did say:
'Where sall we gang and dine the day?'

'In behind yon auld fail dyke
I wot there lies a new-slain knight;
And naebody kens that he lies there
But his hawk, his hound, and his lady fair.

'His hound is to the hunting gane,
His hawk to fetch the wild-fowl hame;
His lady's ta'en another mate,
So we may mak our dinner sweet.

'Ye'll sit on his white hause-bane,
And I'll pick out his bonny blue een;
Wi' ae lock o' his gowden hair
We'll theek our nest when it grows bare.

'Mony a one for him maks mane,
But nane sall ken whar he is gane,
O'er his white banes, where they are bare,
The wind sall blaw for evermair.'

(b)   *Meeting Point*

Time was away and somewhere else,
There were two glasses and two chairs
And two people with the one pulse
(Somebody stopped the moving stairs),
Time was away and somewhere else.

And they were neither up nor down,
The stream's music did not stop
Flowing through heather, limpid brown,
Although they sat in a coffee-shop,
And they were neither up nor down.

The bell was silent in the air
Holding its inverted poise—
Between the clang and clang a flower,
A brazen calyx of no noise:
The bell was silent in the air.

The camels crossed the miles of sand
That stretched around the cups and plates;
The desert was their own, they planned
To portion out the stars and dates:
The camels crossed the miles of sand.

Time was away and somewhere else.
The waiter did not come, the clock
Forgot them and the radio waltz
Came out like water from a rock:
Time was away and somewhere else.

Her fingers flicked away the ash
That bloomed again in tropic trees:
Not caring if the markets crash
When they had forests such as these,
Her fingers flicked away the ash.

God or whatever means the Good
Be praised that time can stop like this,
That what the heart has understood
Can verify in the body's peace
God or whatever means the Good.

Time was away and she was here
And life no longer what it was,
The bell was silent in the air
And all the room a glow because
Time was away and she was here.

LOUIS MACNEICE

2. Write a critical appreciation of this passage in the light of the following:

(i) What is the theme, or purpose, of the passage?

(ii) How is this theme developed, i.e. what are the stages in the progress of the argument?

(iii) How does Shakespeare render this dramatically a per-suasive piece of rhetoric? (Consider these elements: rhythm, diction, imagery, syntax.)

(iv) Bearing in mind H. Coombes's points concerning Blake's poem, how effectively is the *form* and *style* of this passage suited to the *theme*?

Once more unto the breach, dear friends, once more;
Or close the wall up with our English dead:
In peace, there's nothing so becomes a man,
As modest stillness, and humility:
But when the blast of war blows in our ears,
Then imitate the action of the tiger:
Stiffen the sinews, summon up the blood,
Disguise fair nature with hard-favour'd rage:
Then lend the eye a terrible aspect:
Let it pry through the portage of the head,
Like the brass cannon; let the brow o'erwhelm it,
As fearfully as doth a galled rock
O'erhang and jutty his confounded base,

Swill'd with the wild and wasteful ocean.
Now set the teeth, and stretch the nostril wide,
Hold hard the breath, and bend up every spirit
To his full height. On, on, you noblest English,
Whose blood is fet from fathers of war-proof:
Fathers, that like so many Alexanders,
Have in these parts from morn till even fought,
And sheathed their swords, for lack of argument.

Shakespeare, *Henry V*

12. ACCURATE OBSERVATION

POEM: *Consider* by W. H. Auden.
CRITIC: A. Alvarez.

Consider this and in our time
As the hawk sees it or the helmeted airman:
The clouds rift suddenly—look there
At cigarette-end smouldering on a border
At the first garden party of the year.
Pass on, admire the view of the massif
Through plate-glass windows of the Sport Hotel:
Join there the insufficient units
Dangerous, easy, in furs, in uniform
And constellated at reserved tables
Supplied with feelings by an efficient band
Relayed elsewhere to farmers and their dogs
Sitting in kitchens in the stormy fens.

Long ago, supreme Antagonist,
More powerful than the great northern whale
Ancient and sorry at life's limiting defect,
In Cornwall, Mendip, or the Pennine moor
Your comments on the highborn mining-captains,
Found they no answer, made them wish to die
—Lie since in barrows out of harm.
You talk to your admirers every day
By silted harbours, derelict works,
In strangled orchards, and the silent comb
Where dogs have worried or a bird was shot.

Order the ill that they attack at once:
Visit the ports and, interrupting
The leisurely conversation in the bar
Within a stone's throw of the sunlit water,
Beckon your chosen out. Summon
Those handsome and diseased youngsters, those women
Your solitary agents in the country parishes;

And mobilize the powerful forces latent
In soils that make the farmer brutal
In the infected sinus, and the eyes of stoats.
Then, ready, start your rumour, soft
But horrifying in its capacity to disgust
Which, spreading magnified, shall come to be
A polar peril, a prodigious alarm,
Scattering the people, as torn-up paper
Rags and utensils in a sudden gust,
Seized with immeasurable neurotic dread.

Seekers after happiness, all who follow
The convolutions of your simple wish,
It is later than you think; nearer that day
Far other than that distant afternoon
Amid rustle of frocks and stamping feet
They gave the prizes to the ruined boys.
You cannot be away, then, no
Not though you pack to leave within an hour,
Escaping humming down arterial roads:
The date was yours; the prey to fugues,
Irregular breathing and alternate ascendancies
After some haunted migratory years
To disintegrate on an instant in the explosion of mania
Or lapse for ever into a classic fatigue.

The poem reminds me of one of those Elizabethan plays scholars wrangle about—*Doctor Faustus*, for instance. Part of it has genius, part is hack-work. And like *Doctor Faustus*, the two parts have precious little to do with each other. The good bits—they stand out—are almost entirely of one type; their strength is that of accuracy and economy:

> . . . And constellated at reserved tables
> Supplied with feelings by an efficient band
> Relayed elsewhere to farmers and their dogs
> Sitting in kitchens in the stormy fens.

Or most of the last section, particularly:

> . . . that distant afternoon
> Amid rustle of frocks and stamping feet
> They gave the prizes to the ruined boys.

The lines are founded on business-like observation and a wonderful sense of language. When Auden is writing seriously and well there is rarely any question of his liking his subjects; he merely guts them as neatly as a fishwife deals with a herring. Behind his best work is a tradition that reached its peak with:

> Where slumber abbots purple as their wines.

This is not just a gift for destructive criticism; there is relish and vitality in the performance of a writer who is without doubt very clever, and who enjoys the business of using his skill to let in a little air. But still, the strength is in the accuracy of the observation; it is a flair for the telling detail as well as the telling word. If Auden is contemporary (and he seems to me much more 'contemporary' than 'modern', with all that last word, in its best sense, implies of profound originality), he is so in the way a journalist is contemporary. That is, his business is to observe accurately, to present succinctly and to comment. His comment should be pointed, it should be allusive to what is happening there and then, to fashionable ideas and theories; but within these limits it should be easy. The journalist is not, in short, ever called on to think particularly painfully. His business is with the surface of things, not with their real nature. Even Auden's prose, which is very lively and knock-you-down, is a matter of quick and deft juggling with received ideas—from psychology, anthropology, sociology and so on—than any real effort to get at something he knows, however obscurely, for himself. If Pope is on one side of Auden, Alistair Cooke is on the other.

It is also the journalist in him who allows Auden so much freedom of the cliché. Set beside the lines over which he really seems to have taken pains, large stretches of the poem appear to have been botched up with whatever catch-phrases were nearest to hand:

> . . . The insufficient units . . .
> . . . Silted harbours, derelict works . . .
> . . . Scattering the people, as torn-up paper
> Rags and utensils in a sudden gust . . .

They are all phrases from that Thesaurus of Social Abuses which became so thumb-marked during the 'thirties. It is as though Auden had not written the lines at all, but merely compiled them. This is quite another thing from a poet's making, by over-use, a cliché of his own original discoveries, as Wordsworth did in his decline, and as Eliot has done in his 1954 *Ariel Poem*. These at least give you the feeling that they once meant something; if they are no longer fresh, that is because the poet himself has stopped discovering. But Auden's clichés are quite general, stuck on to the scene automatically, and only remotely connected with the poet himself. It is, of course, perfectly possible to inject a little life into a spent phrase; Pound has done so often enough, triumphantly in *Mauberley*. But he only managed it by using them ironically for his own ends. There are no inverted commas, metaphorical or real, around Auden's clichés; they are obviously intended as serious and moving poetry. Just how much they fail and how inert they are, he himself shows:

> By silted harbours, derelict works,
> In strangled orchards, and the silent comb
> Where dogs have worried or a bird was shot.

It is extraordinary how that last line and a half make you attend; a whole area of allusion wakes into life after the lethargy that has gone before. The movement of the verse becomes more subtle; the poet is no longer shifting around the required properties; in fact, he is less describing the actual scene than registering its importance on him. On the evidence of the poetry, I can't really believe that social abuses ever much troubled Auden, though they may at one time have excited him. But he does seem to have had a profound *odi-et-amo* relationship with the tougher squirearchy, who control with real power their tiny estates in the bleaker parts of England. Hence some of Auden's best writing appears in the very early *Paid On Both Sides,* in which, with the aid of *Beowulf,* he raised his passion for private games and his otherwise overworked sense of doom almost to the level of moral statement. It is as though he yearned for authority in action whilst rejecting it in control. And so there is a curious ambivalence in his attitude to money and power; he says they won't do and yet he has a romantic yearning for those graced with them. There was once an exchange between Scott Fitzgerald and Hemingway that has now achieved notoriety: 'The rich,' said Fitzgerald, 'are different from us.' 'Yes,' replied the good democrat, 'they have more money.' Time and again Auden's poetry seems to be repeating these sentiments—but taking both sides at once:

> Dangerous, easy, in furs, in uniform . . .

I can't quite understand how Auden manages to take the inter-national set so seriously. They are self-seeking, superficial and possibly, at best, cunning. But 'dangerous'? Even from the party line they were mere riff-raff to be swept away. Yet somehow the poet has made of them a personal menace.

For Auden is a journalist not only in the type of social observa-tion he can do and in his freedom with the cliché; there is also his sensationalism. This is why the moments of brilliant social com-ment are not apparently enough. There has to be a sort of Q.E.D. structure; society must die of its own disease, a rebellion of some undefined sort must take place, and finally his own personal dis-likes must go under. So in the second section of the poem an enormous machinery of Fate is rumbled into motion, with full Anglo-Saxon trappings and an obscure mythology to go with it (that 'great northern whale', for example; if he is immortal, then he can't be an ordinary whale; whilst Moby Dick, my only other candidate, had his hunting grounds mostly in the southern hemi-sphere). The aim seems to be to create a sort of modern epic, complete with a modern hero—'the hawk . . . or the helmeted airman'—in which heroic action and Fate will combine to purge society. But somehow the social revolution is lost in the nerves. The poem ends not in the triumph of political right, or of any sort of right, but in psychosis:

> To disintegrate on an instant in the explosion of mania
> Or lapse for ever into a classic fatigue.

I am told that Auden believed that the corruption of society was reflected in the nervous disorder of the people. Perhaps. But then the dread and ominousness of social revolution seem to me con-siderably worked up, out of proportion to the incisiveness of the start and not quite à propos of the theme. For what the dissatisfied, the warped and the diseased have to do with the purgation of society is by no means clear. Certainly no political leader would own them. Even the *intellectual* Marxists have always been rather an embarrassment to Moscow.

from *The Shaping Spirit*

COMMENTARY

A. Alvarez finds in this poem 'much freedom of the cliché'. Cliché (French *clicher*, to stereotype) is a trite or hackneyed phrase used where a new original one is needed. A worn-out phrase may be applied in an arresting way, but usually a cliché shows indifference on the part of the user.

PRACTICAL CRITICISM

1. Summarize, in your own words, the criticism of Auden's poem above.

2. Write an appraisal of the following poem, making close reference to details of language, and of thought, attitude and feeling.

> Where the remote Bermudas ride
> In th'ocean's bosom unespied,
> From a small boat, that rowed along,
> The list'ning winds received this song:
>
>   What should we do but sing His praise
> That led us through the wat'ry maze,
> Unto an isle so long unknown,
> And yet far kinder than our own?
> Where He the huge sea-monsters wracks,
> That lift the deep upon their backs,
> He lands us on a grassy stage,
> Safe from the storms' and prelates' rage.
> He gave us this eternal spring,
> Which here enamels everything;
> And sends the fowls to us in care,
> On daily visits through the air.
> He hangs in shades the orange bright,
> Like golden lamps in a green night;
> And does in the pomgranates close
> Jewels more rich than Ormus shows.
> He makes the figs our mouths to meet,
> And throws the melons at our feet;
> But apples plants of such a price,
> No tree could ever bear them twice.
> With cedars, chosen by His hand
> From Lebanon, He stores the land:
> And makes the hollow seas that roar

Proclaim the ambergris on shore.
He cast—of which we rather boast—
The Gospel's pearl upon our coast;
And in these rocks for us did frame
A temple, where to sound His name.
O let our voice His praise exalt,
Till it arrive at Heaven's vault;
Which thence, perhaps, rebounding, may
Echo beyond the Mexique Bay.

Thus sung they, in the English boat,
An holy and a cheerful note;
And all the way, to guide their chime,
With falling oars they kept the time.

                              Marvell, *The Bermuda*

13. RANGE IN IMAGERY, SOUND, TONE, IRONIES

POEM: from *Epistle IV, Of the Use of Riches* by Alexander Pope.
CRITIC: Reuben Arthur Brower.

Before talking of order in this satire, *Of Riches*, we must respond to the variety and be quite sure we are describing an order felt *within* the 'bright diversity' of the poem. The larger continuities must be perceptible in a moment of the liveliest and most varied reading experience. A good test is to read aloud the scene of Timon's dinner, with the summons to the chapel service that precedes it:

> And now the Chapel's silver bell you hear,
> That summons you to all the Pride of Prayer:
> Light quirks of Music, broken and uneven,
> Make the soul dance upon a Jig to Heaven.
> On painted Ceilings you devoutly stare,
> Where sprawl the Saints of Verrio or Laguerre,
> On gilded clouds in fair expansion lie,
> And bring all Paradise before your eye.
> To rest, the Cushion and soft Dean invite,
> Who never mentions Hell to ears polite.
>   But hark! the chiming Clocks to dinner call;
> A hundred footsteps scrape the marble Hall:
> The rich Buffet well-coloured Serpents grace,
> And gaping Tritons spew to wash your face.
> Is this a dinner? this a Genial room?
> No, 'tis a Temple, and a Hecatomb.
> A solemn Sacrifice, performed in state,
> You drink by measure, and to minutes eat.
> So quick retires each flying course, you'd swear
> Sancho's dread Doctor and his Wand were there.
> Between each Act the trembling salvers ring,
> From soup to sweet-wine, and God bless the King,
> In plenty starving, tantalized in state,
> And complaisantly helped to all I hate,

Treated, caressed, and tired, I take my leave,
Sick of his civil Pride from Morn to Eve;
I curse such lavish cost, and little skill,
And swear no Day was ever past so ill.

Reading the lines aloud, we get an impression of constantly
shifting balance as we vary pace and stress and as we modulate
our voices to make changes of tone or to allow for the fulfilment
of sensuous excitements and ironic implications. The special
demands that the passage makes on a reader point directly to its
surprising range and diversity in images, in patterns of sound,
and especially in tones and ironies. Many of these local variations
belong to continuities running through the whole poem.

In imagery—to begin with that pattern—we pass from the
precious sound of the 'silver bell' to the skipping music which
degenerates into 'a jig to heaven'. Next comes a rich impression
of baroque painting, of Michelangeloesque saints against gilded,
billowing clouds. By a remarkable declension we move to the
padded luxury of the chapel seats and the horrid sensation of a
dean who 'gives' to the touch. Next, the large-sounding clocks
are heard in ironic antiphony to the delicate bell, while the
baroque splendours of the ceiling are matched in the rich and
outré ornaments of the marble hall.

Though we constantly hear the cultivated voice of a guide
speaking—rather obliquely—to an audience of equal sophistica-
tion, the scale of tones is certainly more varied than that of the
imagery. What seemed like a polite comment,

And now the Chapel's silver bell you hear,

steps up via a more formal vocabulary and alliteration to a
pompous announcement:

That summons you to all the Pride of Prayer.

The view of the ceiling reaches its climax in a tone of Miltonic
awe,

And bring all Paradise before your eye,

which in fact parodies a line from 'Il Penseroso',

And bring all Heaven before mine eyes.

The oscillations of tone in the next few lines are most wonderful.
The vision of Paradise is gently interrupted by the soothing voice
of the social raconteur,

> To rest, the Cushion and soft Dean invite,

and the exquisite deference of the cleric,

> Who never mentions Hell to ears polite.

His rather cozy tone is shattered by the shout of a herald, 'But
hark!' Following this hint of heroic narrative the solemnity of a
Roman oration is heard in the diction and in the balanced
rhetorical questions and replies of

> Is this a dinner? this a Genial room?
> No, 'tis a Temple, and a Hecatomb.

The formality of balance continuing through most of the lines
that follow offsets the descent to the personal (the only use of 'I'
in the whole poem). In the context of this rather artificial phrasing
another Miltonic parody enters unobtrusively, while the irony of
the allusion is increased by the contrasting personal tone:

> Treated, caressed, and tired, I take my leave,
> Sick of his civil Pride from Morn to Eve;
> I curse such lavish cost, and little skill,
> And swear no Day was ever past so ill.

All of these diverse tones give rise to irony, not only because
they are often incongruous in relation to the events and persons
being described (as in Dryden), but because they clash with one
another. The accent of Roman cultivation is rudely met by back-
stairs vulgarity: 'Tritons spew to wash your face'. But the opposition goes beyond difference of tone: high art clashes with physical
grossness; ornament, with use. Ironic ambiguities continue to
multiply in phrase after phrase. Consider 'fair expansion' in

> Where sprawl the Saints of Verrio or Laguerre,
> On gilded clouds in fair expansion lie,
> And bring all Paradise before your eye.

Read as 'clouds in fair expansion', the phrase suggests the billowy
grandeur of Rubens or Tiepolo. But bigness in this poem is

always reminding us of grossness, and the extraordinary length of the word, especially at this point in the line, also helps to magnify the image. The clouds are overexpanded. If we read 'saints in fair expansion lie' (which is equally possible), 'fair' means something more than pleasing to the eye. It includes the awkwardness of 'sprawl' and the indecency of 'stare'. Sacred art becomes exhibitionism: 'This were Paradise' indeed!

The dance of oppositions, of indescribable variety, continues from here to the end of the scene. The herald's cry ('But hark!') introduces something less than an epic action. The innocent rhetorical questions are answered by the expected 'no' and by a most unexpected statement that adds fresh ironies:

> Is this a dinner? this a Genial room?
> No, 'tis a Temple, and a Hecatomb.

Inversion is the order of the day: too much time for drink, not enough for eating; much food and little to eat; kindness which is hateful; civility which is pride.

The inversions and other clashes of meaning are distinctly heard. Symmetries and inversions of meaning are matched in the order of accents and words. The matching lines of question and reply divide at exactly the same point; the inversion of propriety is expressed with an inversion of words. Similarly, the inversion of times is matched by chiasmus:

> You drink by measure, and to minutes eat.

This line describing the clock-like precision of the ceremony concludes a series of lines of extraordinarily uniform metrical pattern. Their monotonous regularity is appropriately broken by a couplet that must be read almost in a single breath, its one pause coming in a very odd place:

> So quick retires each flying course, you'd swear
> Sancho's dread Doctor and his Wand were there.

There is quite a different surprise in the reverse break of

> To rest, the Cushion and soft Dean invite
> Who never mentions Hell to ears polite.

The eternal sleep is not exactly what we anticipated. But Pope moves quite beyond the couplet pattern in the lines describing the vast magnificence of the painted heaven:

> On painted Ceilings you devoutly stare,
> Where sprawl the Saints of Verrio or Laguerre,
> On gilded clouds in fair expansion lie,
> And bring all Paradise before your eye.

If by now the reader feels more confusion than harmony in the passage, I shall have had a more than ironic success. For it is necessary to register fully the richness—sensuous, tonal, ironic and rhythmic—of Pope's verse, or we shall find it only too easy to bestow on Pope the conventional unity of 'mechanic warblings'.

from *The Fields of Light*

COMMENTARY

R. A. Brower indicates the special demands that the passage makes on us 'especially in tones and ironies'.

Tone is the poet's attitude in the work and also towards the reader. The tone may be humorous, satirical, passionate, sentimental, cynical and so on.

Irony (Greek *eirōneía,* simulated ignorance) developed from the element of concealment and pretence. *Eirōn,* a stock character of Greek comedy, being undersized, resorted to various forms of deception to overcome *alazon,* the braggart captain. In irony there is a contrast between what is said and what is more or less suggested. The reader must perceive the concealed meaning. Verbal irony may be related to ridicule and sarcasm. As sarcasm (literally 'flesh-tearing') is always bitter (as irony need not be) the connection here is slight.

Antony is speaking ironically in *Julius Caesar* when he says:

> Here, under leave of Brutus and the rest—
> For Brutus is an honourable man;
> So are they all, all honourable men—
> Come I to speak in Caesar's funeral.

R. P. Warren's 'Ballad of Billie Potts' is doubly ironical.

PRACTICAL CRITICISM

List carefully the points which R. A. Brower makes in his critical appreciation of the extract from Pope. Then write a detailed criticism of the following passage:

What then remains, but, waving each Extreme,
The tides of Ignorance and Pride to stem?
Neither so rich a treasure to forgo;
Nor proudly seek beyond our power to know:
Faith is not built on disquisitions vain;
The things we must believe are few and plain:
But since men will believe more than they need;
And every man will make himself a Creed,
In doubtful questions 'tis the safest way
To learn what unsuspected Ancients say:
For 'tis not likely we should higher soar
In search of Heav'n than all the Church before;
Nor can we be deceived, unless we see
The Scripture and the Fathers disagree.
If after all, they stand suspected still,
(For no man's Faith depends upon his Will;)
'Tis some Relief, that points not clearly known,
Without much hazard may be let alone:
And, after hearing what our Church can say,
If still our Reason runs another way,
That private Reason 'tis more Just to curb,
Than by Disputes the public Peace disturb:
For points obscure are of small use to learn:
But common quiet is Mankind's concern.

Dryden, *Religio Laici*

14. SYMBOLIC IMAGE

POEM: *A Sonnet* by George Barker.
CRITIC: C. Day Lewis.

We may find it useful here to examine another poem, a sonnet by George Barker, which owes something to Hopkins in its diction: the subject is an actual experience of the poet's—the sight of two men swept overboard in the Mediterranean.

> The seagull, spreadeagled, splayed on the wind,
> Span backwards shrieking, belly facing upward,
> Fled backward with a gimlet in its heart
> To see the two youths swimming hand in hand
> Through green eternity. O swept overboard
> Not could the thirty-foot jaws them part,
> Or the flouncing skirts that swept them over
> Separate what death pronounced was love.
>
> I saw them, the hand flapping like a flag,
> And another like a dolphin with a child
> Supporting him. Was I the shape of Jesus
> When to me hopeward their eyeballs swivelled,
> Saw I was standing in the stance of vague
> Horror; paralysed with mere pity's peace?

The seagull image with which this sonnet opens is extremely brilliant, both symbolic and evocative; the words pick their punches very coolly; the rhythms, which are excellently contrived throughout the whole poem, convey first a resistance to the wind and in the next two lines surrender to it. Our initial impression is a purely physical one—the picture of a seagull swept backwards over the wake of a ship. It is a sight so familiar to us all that the poet is able to take great imaginative liberties with it, yet remain intelligible. When the first impression peeled off, we became aware of another meaning beneath it: the seagull, which 'Span backwards shrieking, belly facing upward', prepares us emotionally for the two men whirled away in the ship's wake. At this point, the phrase 'Fled backward with a gimlet in its heart' introduces a third motif. It contains not only the previous suggestion of a remorseless force skewering the bird and pushing it backwards, but also the idea of anguish—the anguish of one who sees 'the two youths swimming hand in hand through green eternity', and is helpless—the anguish, in fact, of the poet himself 'standing in the stance of vague horror; paralysed with mere pity's peace'. The sharp, precise word 'gimlet' admirably points this double significance.

But after this the poem is not, perhaps, altogether satisfactory. Our attention begins to wander a little, distracted by images which do not tie in so closely to the theme. We admire the way the smooth rhythm of the seagull's recession changes into the choppy rhythms of

> O swept overboard
> Not could the thirty-foot jaws them part,
> Or the flouncing skirts that swept them over
> Separate what death pronounced was love.

But the images for the waves—jaws and flouncing skirts—are gravely dissonant, and they make no contact with the seagull image. And then, in the sestet, we have two more images, equally centrifugal—the 'hand flapping like a flag' and the 'dolphin with a child supporting him'. Now the cause of our dissatisfaction lies, I fancy, in the poet's failure to maintain the ambivalence so beautifully created by the opening lines. He is trying to be in two places at once, in the consciousness of the drowning men who see him as 'the shape of Jesus', and at the core of his own experience as a witness of their fate. The poem, attempting thus to look outwards and inwards at the same time, becomes emotionally unfocused: we do not doubt the intensity of the poet's experience; but we find that the pure, subjective images rising from the inwardness of this experience do not perfectly fuse with the images which are intended to convey its external cause. . . . It is at least sufficiently impure to admit one direct statement or piece of poetic argument—that the waves could not 'Separate what death pronounced was love'.

from *The Poetic Image*

COMMENTARY

When C. Day Lewis says above, 'in the sestet, we have two more images equally centrifugal' he means that each image is tending to fly away from the centre, from the main theme of the poem. If you examine a sonnet by Shakespeare, Milton, Wordsworth or Keats you will find that the images support one another and hold the poem together. The sequence and structure of some poems depend upon a single dominant image.

See David Daiches, *A Study of Literature,* Chapter 7.

PRACTICAL CRITICISM

Elucidate, as far as you can, the meaning of the following poem, giving close attention to the details of its expression:

Mr Bleaney

'This was Mr Bleaney's room. He stayed
The whole time he was at the Bodies, till
They moved him.' Flowered curtains, thin and frayed,
Fall to within five inches of the sill,

Whose window shows a strip of building land,
Tussocky, littered. 'Mr Bleaney took
My bit of garden properly in hand.'
Bed, upright chair, sixty-watt bulb, no hook

Behind the door, no room for books or bags—
'I'll take it.' So it happens that I lie
Where Mr Bleaney lay, and stub my fags
On the same saucer-souvenir, and try

Stuffing my ears with cotton-wool, to drown
The jabbering set he egged her on to buy.
I know his habits—what time he came down,
His preference for sauce to gravy, why

He kept on plugging at the four aways—
Likewise their yearly frame: the Frinton folk
Who put him up for summer holidays,
And Christmas at his sister's house in Stoke.

But if he stood and watched the frigid wind
Tousling the clouds, lay on the fusty bed
Telling himself that this was home, and grinned,
And shivered, without shaking off the dread

That how we live measures our own nature,
And at his age having no more to show
Than one hired box should make him pretty sure
He warranted no better, I don't know.

PHILIP LARKIN

15. PERSONAL FEELING

POEM: *Do Not Go Gentle Into That Good Night* by Dylan Thomas.
CRITIC: Archibald MacLeish.

Poems are made by men and if men cannot undertake to comprehend their making, then poems are smaller not greater, weaker not stronger, on that account. Anyone, I submit, who will begin, not with talk about poetry but with poetry itself, can make his way to conclusions of a kind and even, conceivably, to conclusions he can accept as true.

Begin, therefore, with a poem—borrow an axe-handle as a pattern for the axe-handle you are about to attempt to hew. The poem I should suggest is one not only famous in itself but famous in the author's reading of it, for the author was, in my judgment at least, the finest reader of his own work of whom we have record: Dylan Thomas's *Do Not Go Gentle Into That Good Night.*

> Do not go gentle into that good night,
> Old age should burn and rave at close of day;
> Rage, rage against the dying of the light.
>
> Though wise men at their end know dark is right,
> Because their words have forked no lightning they
> Do not go gentle into that good night.
>
> Good men, the last wave by, crying how bright
> Their frail deeds might have danced in a green bay,
> Rage, rage against the dying of the light.
>
> Wild men who caught and sang the sun in flight,
> And learn, too late, they grieved it on its way,
> Do not go gentle into that good night.
>
> Grave men, near death, who see with blinding sight
> Blind eyes could blaze like meteors and be gay,
> Rage, rage against the dying of the light.

And you, my father, there on the sad height,
Curse, bless, me now with your fierce tears, I pray.
Do not go gentle into that good night.
Rage, rage against the dying of the light.

I think we can probably agree that this poem is a trap and cage in which a heaven and earth we recognize is somehow caught. A boy's agony, face to face with the humility and submission of a dying father, is held here in such a way that we not only know the pain but know also something we had not known before about that mysterious turning away which is the cause of pain. But can we go further still? Can we say *how* this knowing is given to us?

We can take, I think, at least one step. We can agree that whatever it is we know in this poem, we know only *in* the poem. It is not a knowledge we can extract from the poem like a meat from a nut and carry off. It is something the *poem* means—something that is gone when the poem goes and recovered only by returning to the poem's words. And not only by returning to the poem's words but by returning to them within the poem. If we alter them, if we change their order, though leaving their sense much as it is, if we speak them so that their movement changes, their meaning changes also.

This far, we can surely go together, for the simplest experiment will prove these statements true. But can we go beyond this? Can we say how it is that these words in this order and moving to this movement have the power to contain a meaning which can so easily be lost and which cannot elsewhere be found? These words of Dylan Thomas's are very ordinary words—in no way remarkable. They are grouped in simple sentences. There is nothing unusual about them in any way—nothing fantastic or violent or particularly memorable even. And yet we know what they can do because they have done it. What explanation can we give ourselves?

Well, there is a question we can ask which will perhaps give us a direction in which to look. Simple and familiar as they are, is there nothing unusual about these words as words-in-the-poem? Are they in no way different there from the same words in a paragraph of prose—in no way different from the same words arranged in the order and pattern of a paragraph of prose? Obviously, as I think you will agree, they are different. They seem to have what

I can only call, for myself, more *weight* than the same words have
when we run across them in ordinary conversation or on the page
of a newspaper or even on a page of prose. There is an enhancement of their meanings, or perhaps, more precisely, of the significance of their meanings. It is not an enhancement which can be
defined by abstract analysis and measurement. But the inability to
define in abstract terms does not mean, contrary to notions now in
vogue, that an experience is fanciful. It is still possible, even under
the new vocabulary, to feel as well as to define. And what is
present here is *felt*.

The words of the poem have—have inescapably when placed in
the poem and in the author's voicing of the poem—a sense of
signifying something 'more'—the kind of look a familiar face may
have when head turns, eyes meet, in an unexpected way—the kind
of look a familiar landscape takes on in a sidewise light. This 'rage'
of Dylan's is not the rage one sees in a child in tantrums or a
mother crossed or even in an Alexander in a play. This 'dying of
the light' is not a mere diminishment at evening. This 'good night'
is neither 'good' nor 'night' nor yet a simple saying of farewell but
all of them together and much more than all. Emotion *knows* the
difference even though mind is defeated in its busy effort to pinch
the difference between the thumb and finger of reason and so dispose of it. Emotion—and this is perhaps the point precisely—
cannot dispose of it. Emotion stands there staring.

Ezra Pound has a wonderful phrase about good writing which,
because Pound is a poet, is really applicable to poetry alone. He
talks about each and every word being 'charged with meaning'.
That is what has happened here. These words are charged with
meaning in the poem as they are not charged with meaning outside
it. Or rather they are charged, in the poem, with a particular kind
of meaning: a meaning which goes straight to what we call the
heart—intending by that term the organ of intelligence which
takes its meanings whole and live, not masticated into chewed
abstractions. But how are they so charged? Or is this the question
one cannot ask, because it is the question which attempts to pick
the lock of the secret of the creative act? Or can we ask it? Can we
ask it in humility and patience, leaving the poem to reply?

Return for a moment and read the simple words of the poem
again. Read them simply, letting them take their sure positions
within the structure which contains them. You will see—have
already seen—what some of the formal relationships are. They

are very obvious. They can even be stated in statistical terms. For one thing, the words are arranged in a grammatical order as words are in ordinary compositions. Here, there are eight sentences, each of them simple in form—imperative or declarative. But it is not only these sentences which hold the words together. They are also held in another kind of structure: a structure the elements of which have nothing to do with sentences or syntax but with something which sentences and syntax regard as irrelevant and fortuitous—the *sounds* the words make in the mouth and in the ear when they are spoken—the accenting or unaccenting of their syllables—the sounds of their letters, both consonants and vowels. They are arranged, first of all, in 'lines', nineteen in all, each 'line' consisting of ten syllables, five accented and five not. These 'lines', in turn, are so arranged that they end in words which, as we say, 'rhyme'. The rhymes, again, are two in number based on 'night' and 'day', the first rhyme appearing thirteen times and the second six, in a regular pattern. Finally—though this does not exhaust the elements of construction—two of the lines are repeated four times each. These statistics may be impertinent and annoying but the structure they describe is obviously neither. It is a structure deliberately and purposefully composed of words as sounds, or, more precisely, of the repetitions of words as sounds. Now the question is: is there a relationship between this structure and the capacity of the poem to mean?—the capacity of the words to mean more than their ordinary meanings?

Manifestly there is. I say manifestly because it is only this structure which distinguishes the relationships of these familiar words in their familiar order from their usual relationships in the sentences and syntax of prose. But does it follow—and this is, of course, the essential question—does it follow that it is *because* and solely because of the structure of the words as sounds that the meaning of the words as meaning is enhanced? One of the greatest poets of the last century and one of the most intellectually precise and articulate minds of many centuries apparently thought so. Writing to Degas in a famous letter Stéphane Mallarmé gave it as his flat and considered opinion that poetry is made not with ideas but with words. Since ideas are expressed in words and cannot very well exist without them, and since many words signify ideas whether we wish them to or not, this statement must be taken to mean that poetry is made not with words-as-expressions-of-ideas but with what Mallarmé elsewhere called 'words themselves', words as sensuous events—in brief, words as the sounds that convey them.

What this assertion comes down to then—the assertion that poetry is made not with 'ideas' but with 'words'—what it comes down to is the proposition that it is exclusively in the relationships of words as sounds that the poem as poem exists. The poem's meaning is evoked by the structure of words-as-sounds rather than by the structure of words-as-meanings. And the enhancement of meaning, which we feel in any true poem, is a product, therefore, of the structure of the sounds.

from *Poetry and Experience*

COMMENTARY

In the critical passage above, we are told that Ezra Pound has a wonderful phrase about good writing and talks about 'each and every word being charged with meaning'. MacLeish goes on to show us how this applies most convincingly to poetry.

In close reading, therefore, we must consider everything that a word can do—in meaning (combining thought and feeling), sound and association. This, with the ordering of the rhythm, leads to the total meaning of the poem.

PRACTICAL CRITICISM

Discuss the salient points which emerge from MacLeish's assessment of the poem by Dylan Thomas.

Bearing these in mind, write a detailed appraisal of each of the following:

(i)   Thus with the Year
Seasons return, but not to me returns
Day, or the sweet approach of Ev'n or Morn,
Or sight of vernal bloom, or Summers Rose,
Or flocks, or herds, or human face divine;
But cloud in stead, and ever-during dark
Surrounds me, from the cheerful ways of men
Cut off, and for the Book of Knowledge fair
Presented with a Universal blank

Of Natures works to me expung'd and ras'd,
And wisdom at one entrance quite shut out.
So much the rather thou Celestial light
Shine inward, and the mind through all her powers
Irradiate, there plant eyes, all mist from thence
Purge and disperse, that I may see and tell
Of things invisible to mortal sight.

MILTON

(ii)
      Adieu, farewell earth's bliss,
      This world uncertain is;
      Fond are life's lustful joys,
      Death proves them all but toys,
      None from his darts can fly.
      I am sick, I must die.
          Lord have mercy on us!

      Rich men, trust not in wealth,
      Gold cannot buy you health;
      Physic himself must fade,
      All things to end are made.
      The plague full swift goes by;
      I am sick, I must die.
          Lord have mercy on us!

      Beauty is but a flower
      Which wrinkles will devour;
      Brightness falls from the air,
      Queens have died young and fair,
      Dust hath closed Helen's eye.
      I am sick, I must die.
          Lord have mercy on us!

      Strength stoops unto the grave,
      Worms feed on Hector brave,
      Swords may not fight with fate.
      Earth still holds ope her gate;
      Come! come! the bells do cry.
      I am sick, I must die.
          Lord have mercy on us!

Wit with his wantonness
Tasteth death's bitterness;
Hell's executioner
Hath no ears for to hear
What vain art can reply.
I am sick, I must die.
    Lord have mercy on us!

Haste, therefore, each degree,
To welcome destiny.
Heaven is our heritage,
Earth but a player's stage;
Mount we unto the sky.
I am sick, I must die.
    Lord have mercy on us!

THOMAS NASHE

There came a wind like a bugle;
It quivered through the grass,
And a green chill upon the heat
So ominous did pass
We barred the windows and the doors
As from an emerald ghost;
The doom's electric moccasin
That very instant passed.
On a strange mob of panting trees,
And fences fled away,

And rivers where the houses ran
The living looked that day.
The bell within the steeple wild
The flying tidings whirled.
How much can come
And much can go,
And yet abide the world!

EMILY DICKINSON

(iv)   The world is charged with the grandeur of God.
    It will flame out, like shining from shook foil;
    It gathers to a greatness, like the ooze of oil
Crushed. Why do men then now not reck his rod?

Generations have trod, have trod, have trod;
   And all is seared with trade; bleared, smeared with toil;
   And wears man's smudge and shares man's smell: the soil
Is bare now, nor can foot feel, being shod.

And for all this, nature is never spent;
   There lives the dearest freshness deep down things;
And though the last lights off the black West went
   Oh, morning, at the brown brink eastward, springs—
Because the Holy Ghost over the bent
   World broods with warm breast and with ah! bright wings.

                  GERARD MANLEY HOPKINS

II
Passages for
Close Reading

*A number of signed and unsigned poems
and passages of poetry,
some grouped for contrast and comparison*

PASSAGES WITH QUESTIONS

1. Compare and contrast the following poems:

(a)   *The Viper*

> Barefoot I went and made no sound;
> The earth was hot beneath:
> The air was quivering around,
> The circling kestrel eyed the ground
> And hung above the heath.
>
> There in the pathway stretched along
> The lovely serpent lay:
> She reared not up the heath among,
> She bowed her head, she sheathed her tongue,
> And shining stole away.
>
> Fair was the brave embroidered dress,
> Fairer the gold eyes shone:
> Loving her not, yet did I bless
> The fallen angel's comeliness;
> And gazed when she had gone.

RUTH PITTER

(b)   *Beagles*

> Over rock and wrinkled ground
> Ran the lingering nose of hound,
> The little and elastic hare
> Stretched herself nor stayed to stare.
>
> Stretched herself, and far away
> Darted through the chinks of day,
> Behind her, shouting out her name,
> The whole blind world galloping came.
>
> Over hills a running line
> Curled like a whip-lash, fast and fine,
> Past me sailed the sudden pack
> Along the taut and tingling track.

From the far·flat scene each shout
Like jig-saw piece came tumbling out,
I took and put them all together
And then they turned into a tether.

A tether that held me to the hare
Here, there and everywhere.

W. R. RODGERS

2. Analyse and compare the following passages as examples of Shakespeare's dramatic verse:

(a)   All furnish'd, all in arms;
All plumed like estridges that with the wind
Bated like eagles having lately bathed;
Glittering in golden coats, like images;
As full of spirit as the month of May,
And gorgeous as the sun at midsummer;
Wanton as youthful goats, wild as young bulls.
I saw young Harry, with his beaver on,
His cuisses on his thighs, gallantly arm'd,
Rise from the ground like feather'd Mercury,
And vaulted with such ease into his seat,
As if an angel dropp'd down from the clouds,
To turn and wind a fiery Pegasus,
And witch the world with noble horsemanship.

(b)   You sin against
Obedience, which you owe your father. For
The contract you pretend with that base wretch,
One bred of alms and foster'd with cold dishes,
With scraps o' th' court—it is no contract, none.
And though it be allowed in meaner parties—
Yet who than he more mean?—to knit their souls—
On whom there is no more dependency
But brats and beggary—in self-figur'd knot,
Yet you are curb'd from that enlargement by
The consequence o' th' crown, and must not foil

The precious note of it with a base slave,
A hilding for a livery, a squire's cloth,
A pantler—not so eminent!

(c)   I am the man. If it be so—as 'tis—
Poor lady, she were better love a dream.
Disguise, I see thou wert a wickedness
Wherein the pregnant enemy does much.
How easy is it for the proper-false
In women's waxen hearts to set their forms!
Alas, our frailty is the cause, not we!
For such as we are made of, such we be.
How will this fadge? My master loves her dearly,
And I, poor monster, fond as much on him:
And she, mistaken, seems to dote on me.

3. Giving your reasons clearly, assess the merits of the following
poems:

(a)   I know some lonely houses off the road
A robber'd like the look of,—
Wooden barred,
And windows hanging low,
Inviting to
A portico,

Where two could creep:
One hand the tools,
The other peep
To make sure all's asleep.
Old-fashioned eyes
Not easy to surprise!

How orderly the kitchen'd look by night
With just a clock,—
But they could gag the tick,
And mice won't bark;
And so the walls don't tell,
None will.

A pair of spectacles ajar just stir—
An almanac's aware.
Was it the mat winked,
Or a nervous star?
The moon slides down the stair
To see who's there.

There's plunder,—where?
Tankard, or spoon,
Earring, or stone,
A watch, some ancient brooch
To match the grandmamma
Staid sleeping there.

Day rattles, too,
Stealth's slow;
The sun has got as far
As the third sycamore.
Screams chanticleer,
'Who's there?'

And echoes, trains away,
Sneer—'Where?'
While the old couple, just astir,
Think that the sunrise left the door ajar!

(b) Magdalen at Michael's gate
    Tirlèd at the pin
  On Joseph's thorn sang the blackbird,
    'Let her in! Let her in!'

  'Hast thou seen the wounds?' said Michael,
    'Know'st thou thy sin?'
  'It is evening, evening,' sang the blackbird,
    'Let her in! Let her in!'

  'Yes, I have seen the wounds,
    And I know my sin.'
  'She knows it well, well, well,' sung the blackbird,
    'Let her in! Let her in!'

'Thou bringest no offerings,' said Michael.
　'Nought save sin.'
And the blackbird sang, 'She is sorry, sorry, sorry,
　'Let her in! Let her in!'

When he had sung himself to sleep,
　And night did begin,
One came and open'd Michael's gate,
　And Magdalen went in.

4. Compare and contrast the following sonnets:

(*a*)　O Nightingale, that on yon bloomy Spray
　　Warbl'st at eeve, when all the Woods are still,
　　Thou with fresh hope the Lovers heart dost fill,
　　While the jolly hours lead on propitious May,
Thy liquid notes that close the eye of Day,
　　First heard before the shallow Cuccoo's bill
　　Portend success in Love; O if Jove's will
　　Have linkt that amorous power to thy soft lay,
Now timely sing, ere the Rude bird of Hate
　　Foretell my hopeless doom in som Grove ny:
　　As thou from yeer to yeer hast sung too late
For my relief; yet hadst no reason why,
　　Whether the Muse, or Love call thee his mate,
　　Both them I serve, and of their train am I.

(*b*)　O Friend! I know not which way I must look
　　For comfort, being, as I am, opprest,
　　To think that now our Life is only drest
　　For shew; mean handywork of craftsman, cook
Or groom! We must run glittering like a Brook
　　In the open sunshine, or we are unblest:
　　The wealthiest man among us is the best:
　　No grandeur now in nature or in book
Delights us. Rapine, avarice, expence,
　　This is idolatry; and these we adore:
　　Plain living and high thinking are no more:

The homely beauty of the good old cause
Is gone; our peace, our fearful innocence,
And pure religion breathing household laws.

(c)   Whoso list to hunt? I know where is an hind!
But as for me, alas! I may no more,
The vain travail hath wearied me so sore;
I am of them that furthest come behind.
Yet may I by no means my wearied mind,
Draw from the deer; but as she fleeth afore
Fainting I follow; I leave off therefore,
Since in a net I seek to hold the wind.
Who list her hunt, I put him out of doubt
As well as I, may spend his time in vain!
And graven with diamonds in letters plain,
There is written her fair neck round about;
    'Noli me tangere; for Caesar's I am,
    And wild for to hold, though I seem tame.'

(d) Look at the stars! look, look up at the skies!
    O look at all the fire-folk sitting in the air!
    The bright boroughs, the circle-citadels there!
Down in dim woods the diamond delves! the elves'-eyes!
The grey lawns cold where gold, where quickgold lies!
    Wind-beat whitebeam! airy abeles set on a flare!
    Flake-doves sent floating forth at a farmyard scare!
Ah well! it is all a purchase, all a prize.
Buy then! bid then! What? Prayer, patience, alms, vows.
Look, look: a May-mess, like on orchard boughs!
    Look! March-bloom, like on mealed-with-yellow sallows!
These are indeed the barn; withindoors house
The shocks. This piece-bright paling shuts the spouse
Christ home, Christ and his mother and all his hallows.

(e) That selfe same tonge which first did thee entreat
To linke thy liking with my lucky love:
That trustie tonge must nowe these wordes repeate,
I love thee still, my fancie cannot move.

That dreadlesse hart which durst attempt the thought
To win thy will with mine for to consent,
Maintaines that vow which love in me first wrought,
I *love thee still*, and never shall repent.
That happie hande which hardely did touch,
Thy tender body to my deepe delight:
Shall serve with sword to prove my passion such
As loves thee still, much more than it can write.
Thus love I still with tongue, hand, hart and all,
And when I chaunge, let vengeance on me fall.

5. Examine the following passages from Shakespeare and describe
each briefly in terms of diction, imagery, rhythm, tone and the
general effect to which these contribute.

(*a*) All places that the eye of heaven visits
     Are to a wise man ports and happy havens.
     Teach thy necessity to reason thus:
     There is no virtue like necessity.
     Think not the King did banish thee,
     But thou the King. Woe doth the heavier sit
     Where it perceives it is but faintly borne.
     Go, say I sent thee forth to purchase honour,
     And not the King exil'd thee; or suppose
     Devouring pestilence hangs in our air
     And thou art flying to a fresher clime.
     Look what thy soul holds dear, imagine it
     To lie that way thou goest, not whence thou com'st.
     Suppose the singing birds musicians,
     The grass whereon thou tread'st the presence strew'd.
     The flowers fair ladies, and thy steps no more
     Than a delightful measure or a dance;
     For gnarling sorrow hath less power to bite
     The man that mocks at it and sets it light.

(*b*) Now for our mountain sport. Up to yond hill;
     Your legs are young; I'll tread these flats. Consider,
     When you above perceive me like a crow,

That it is place which lessens and sets off;
And you may then revolve what tales I have told you
Of courts, of princes, of the tricks in war;
This service is not service, so being done,
But being so allow'd; to apprehend thus
Draws us a profit from all things we see,
And often, to our comfort, shall we find
The sharded beetle in a safer hold
Than is the full-wing'd eagle. Oh! this life
Is nobler than attending for a check,
Richer than doing nothing for a bribe,
Prouder than rustling in unpaid-for silk;
Such gain the cap of him that makes 'em fine,
Yet keeps his book uncross'd; no life to ours.

(c)   Not that I think you did not love your father;
But that I know love is begun by time;
And that I see, in passages of proof,
Time qualifies the spark and fire of it.
There lives within the very flame of love
A kind of wick or snuff that will abate it;
And nothing is at a like goodness still;
For goodness, growing to a pleurisy,
Dies in his own too much. That we would do,
We should do when we would; for this 'would' changes,
And hath abatements and delays as many
As there are tongues, are hands, are accidents;
And then this 'should' is like a spendthrift's sigh,
That hurts by easing.

(d)   Merely, thou art Death's fool;
For him that labour'st by thy flight to shun
And yet run'st toward him still. Thou art not noble;
For all th' accommodations that thou bear'st
Are nurs'd by baseness. Thou'rt by no means valiant;
For thou dost fear the soft and tender fork
Of a poor worm. Thy best of rest is sleep,
And that thou oft provok'st; yet grossly fear'st
Thy death, which is no more. Thou art not thyself;

For thou exist'st on many a thousand grains
That issue out of dust. Happy thou art not;
For what thou hast not, still thou striv'st to get,
And what thou hast, forget'st. Thou art not certain;
For thy complexion shifts to strange effects,
After the moon.

6. Discuss the metrical characteristics of each of the following:

(*a*)   I bow my head in silence, I make haste
         Alone, I make haste out into the dark,
         My life and youth and hope all run to waste.
     Is this my body cold and stiff and stark,
         Ashes made ashes, earth becoming earth,
         Is this a prize for man to make his mark?
     Am I that very I who laughed in mirth
         A while ago, a little little while,
         Yet all the while a-dying since my birth?
     Now am I tired, too tired to strive or smile;
         I sit alone, my mouth is in the dust:
         Look thou upon me, Lord, for I am vile.

(*b*)   See how the World its Veterans rewards!
     A Youth of Frolics, an old Age of Cards,
     Fair to no purpose, artful to no end,
     Young without Lovers, old without a Friend;
     A Fop their Passion, but their Prize a Sot;
     Alive, ridiculous, and dead, forgot!

(*c*) Thou hast conquered, O pale Galilean; the world has
     grown grey from thy breath;
     We have drunken of things Lethean, and fed on the
     fullness of death.
     Laurel is green for a season, and love is sweet for a day;
     But love grows bitter with treason, and laurel outlives
     not May.

(d)   Bid me to live, and I will live
          Thy Protestant to be:
        Or bid me love, and I will give
          A loving heart to thee.

        A heart as soft, a heart as kind,
          A heart as sound and free,
        As in the whole world thou canst find,
          That heart Ile give to thee.

        Bid that heart stay, and it will stay,
          To honour thy Decree:
        Or bid it languish quite away
          And't shall doe so for thee.

(e)   Is out with it! oh,
        We lash with the best or worst
       Word last! How a lush-kept plush-capped sloe
        Will, mouthed to flesh-burst,
     Gush!—flush the man, the being with it, sour or sweet,
      Brim, in a flash, full!—Hither then, last or first,
        To hero of Calvary, Christ's feet—
Never ask if meaning it, wanting it, warned of it—men go.

7. Write a critical appreciation of this poem.

Old Woman

So much she caused she cannot now account for
As she stands watching day return, the cool
Walls of the house moving towards the sun.
She puts some flowers in a vase and thinks
    'There is not much I can arrange
In here and now, but flowers are suppliant

As children never were. And love is now
A flicker of memory, my body is
My own entirely. When I lie at night
I gather nothing now into my arms,
    No child or man, and where I live
Is what remains when men and children go.'

Yet she owns more than residue of lives
That she has marked and altered. See how she
Warns time from too much touching her possessions
By keeping flowers fed, by polishing
    Her fine old silver. Gratefully
She sees her own glance printed on grandchildren.

Drawing the curtains back and opening windows
Every morning now, she feels her years
Grow less and less. Time puts no burden on
Her now she does not need to measure it.
    It is acceptance she arranges
And her own life she places in the vase.

ELIZABETH JENNINGS

8. Explain the meaning of this poem, and comment on its form
   and its diction.

Autumn Chapter in a Novel

Through woods, Mme Une Telle, a trifle ill
With idleness, but no less beautiful,
Walks with the young tutor, round their feet
Mob syllables slurred to a fine complaint,
Which in their time held off the natural heat.

The sun is distant, and they fill out space
Sweatless as watercolour under glass.
He kicks abruptly. But we may suppose
The leaves he scatters thus will settle back
In much the same position as they rose.

A tutor's indignation works on air,
Altering nothing; action bustles where,
Towards the pool by which they lately stood,
The husband comes discussing with his bailiff
Poachers, the broken fences round the wood.

Pighead! The poacher is at large, and lingers,
A dead mouse gripped between his sensitive fingers:
Fences already keep the live game out:
See how your property twists her parasol,
Hesitates in the tender trap of doubt.

Here they repair, here daily handle lightly
The brief excitements that disturb them nightly;
Sap draws back inch by inch, and to the ground
The words they uttered rustle constantly:
Silent, they watch the growing, weightless mound.

They leave at last a chosen element,
Resume the motions of their discontent;
She takes her sewing up, and he again
Names to her son the deserts on the globe,
And leaves thrust violently upon the pane.

THOM GUNN

9. Make a critical comparison of the following, examining the
means of expression used by each of the two poets, and
estimating the success of each:

(a)   Hearke, now every thing is still—
       The Screech-Owle, and the whistler shrill,
       Call upon our Dame, aloud,
       And bid her quickly don her shrowd:
       Much you had of Land and rent,
       Your length in clay's now competent.
       A long war disturb'd your minde,
       Here your perfect peace is sign'd—
       Of what is't fooles make such vaine keeping?
       Sin their conception, their birth, weeping:

Their life, a generall mist of error,
Their death, a hideous storme of terror—
Strewe your haire, with powders sweete:
Don cleane linnen, bathe your feete,
And (the foule fiend more to checke)
A crucifixe let blesse your necke,
'Tis now full tide, 'tweene night, and day,
End your groane, and come away.

(b) Prayer the Churches banquet, Angels age,
    Gods breath in man returning to his birth,
  The soul in paraphrase, heart in pilgrimage,
    The Christian plummet sounding heav'n and earth;

  Engine against th'Almightie, sinners towre,
    Reversed thunder, Christ-side-piercing spear,
  The six-daies-world-transposing in an houre,
    A kind of tune, which all things heare and fear;

  Softnesse, and peace, and joy, and love, and blisse,
    Exalted Manna, gladnesse of the best,
    Heaven in ordinarie, man well drest,
  The milkie way, the bird of Paradise,

    Church-bells beyond the starres heard, the souls blood,
    The land of spices, something understood.

10. In four different plays conspirators speak the following
    passages. Show how Shakespeare reveals the working of the
    conspirator's mind and suggests the motives.

(a)   He would be crown'd:
    How that might change his nature, there's the question:
    It is the bright day that brings forth the adder,
    And that craves wary walking. Crown him?—that—
    And then, I grant, we put a sting in him
    That at his will he may do danger with.
    The abuse of greatness is when it disjoins
    Remorse from power; and, to speak truth of Caesar,

I have not known when his affections sway'd
More than his reason. But 'tis a common proof,
That lowliness is young ambition's ladder,
Whereto the climber-upward turns his face;
But when he once attains the upmost round,
He then unto the ladder turns his back,
Looks in the clouds, scorning the base degrees
By which he did ascend: so Caesar may;
Then, lest he should, prevent. And since the quarrel
Will bear no colour for the thing he is,
Fashion it thus; that what he is, augmented,
Would run to these and these extremities:
And therefore think him as a serpent's egg
Which hatch'd would as his kind grow mischievous,
And kill him in the shell.

(b)   The king is weary
Of dainty and such picking grievances,
For he hath found to end one doubt by death
Revives two greater in the heirs of life;
And therefore he will wipe his tables clean,
And keep no tell-tale to his memory
That may repeat and history his loss
To new remembrance; for full well he knows
He cannot so precisely weed this land
As his misdoubts present occasion:
His foes are so enrooted with his friends,
That, plucking to unfix an enemy,
He doth unfasten so and shake a friend.
So that this land, like an offensive wife
That hath enraged him on to offer strokes,
As he is striking, holds his infant up,
And hangs resolved correction in the arm
That was upreared to execution.

(c)   Let's further think of this;
Weigh what convenience both of time and means
May fit us to our shape. If this should fail,
And that our drift look through our bad performance,
'Twere better not assay'd: therefore this project

Should have a back or second, that might hold
If this did blast in proof. Soft, let me see,
We'll make a solemn wager on your cunnings—
I ha't!
When in your motions you are hot and dry—
As make your bouts more violent to that end—
And that he calls for drink, I'll have prepared him
A chalice for the nonce; whereon but sipping,
If he by chance escape your venom'd stuck,
Our purpose may hold there.

(d)   And then for her
To win the Moor—were't to renounce his baptism,
All seals and symbols of redeemed sin—
His soul is so enfetter'd to her love
That she may make, unmake, do what she list,
Even as her appetite shall play the god
With his weak function. How am I, then, a villain
To counsel Cassio to this parallel course,
Directly to his good? Divinity of hell!
When devi's will their blackest sins put on,
They do suggest at first with heavenly shows,
As I do now; for whiles this honest fool
Plies Desdemona to repair his fortunes,
And she for him pleads strongly to the Moor,
I'll pour this pestilence into his ear—
That she repeals him for her body's lust;
And by how much she strives to do him good
She shall undo her credit with the Moor.
So will I turn her virtue into pitch;
And out of her own goodness make the net
That shall enmesh them all.

11. Comment on the meaning, intention, tone and diction of this
poem.

Ghosts

The terrace is said to be haunted.
By whom or what nobody knows; someone

Put away under the vines behind dusty glass
And rusty hinges staining the white-framed door
Like a nosebleed, locked; or a death in the pond
In three feet of water, a courageous breath?
It's haunted anyway, so nobody mends it
And the paving lies loose for the ants to crawl through
Weaving and clutching like animated thorns.
We walk on to it,
Like the bold lovers we are, ten years of marriage,
Tempting the ghosts out with our high spirits,
Footsteps doubled by the silence. . . .

. . . . and start up like ghosts ourselves
Flawed lank and drawn in the greenhouse glass:
She turns from that, and I sit down,
She tosses the dust with the toe of a shoe,
Sits on the pond's parapet and takes a swift look
At her shaking face in the clogged water,
Weeds in her hair; rises quickly and looks at me.
I shrug, and turn my palms out, begin
To feel the damp in my bones as I lever up
And step toward her with my hints of wrinkles,
Crows-feet and shadows. We leave arm in arm
Not a word said. The terrace is haunted,
Like many places with rough mirrors now,
By estrangement, if the daylight's strong.

PETER REDGROVE

12. Examine the following passages of dramatic verse from
Shakespeare and describe each in terms of diction, imagery,
rhythm, tone and the general effect to which these contribute.

(*a*) In the corrupted currents of this world
Offence's gilded hand may shove by justice,
And oft 'tis seen the wicked prize itself
Buys out the law; but 'tis not so above;
There is no shuffling, there the action lies
In his true nature, and we ourselves compell'd
Even to the teeth and forehead of our faults

To give in evidence. What then? what rests?
Try what repentance can: what can it not?
Yet what can it, when one can not repent?
O wretched state! O bosom black as death!
O limed soul, that, struggling to be free
Art more engaged! Help, angels! make assay;
Bow, stubborn knees; and heart with strings of steel
Be soft as sinews of the new-born babe.
All may be well.

(*b*)   What you do
Still betters what is done. When you speak, sweet,
I'd have you do it ever: when you sing,
I'd have you buy and sell so; so give alms;
Pray so; and, for the ordering your affairs,
To sing them too: when you do dance, I wish you
A wave o' the sea, that you might ever do
Nothing but that; move still, still so,
And own no other function: each your doing,
So singular in each particular,
Crowns what you are doing in the present deed,
That all your acts are queens.

PASSAGES WITHOUT QUESTIONS

1. A man so various that he seemed to be
Not one, but all mankind's epitome.
Stiff in opinions, always in the wrong;
Was everything by starts, and nothing long;
But, in the course of one revolving moon,
Was chemist, fiddler, statesman and buffoon:
Then all for women, painting, rhyming, drinking:
Besides ten thousand freaks that died in thinking.
Blest madman, who could every hour employ,
With something new to wish, or to enjoy!
Railing and praising were his usual themes;
And both (to show his judgement) in extremes:
So over violent, or over civil,
That every man, with him, was god or devil.
In squandering wealth was his peculiar art:
Nothing went unrewarded, but desert.
Beggared by fools, whom still he found too late:
He had his jest, and they had his estate.

Dryden, On the Duke of Buckingham

2. When God at first made man,
Having a glass of blessings standing by—
Let us (said he) pour on him all we can;
Let the world's riches, which dispersed lie,
 Contract into a span.

So strength first made a way,
Then beauty flow'd, then wisdom, honour, pleasure:
When almost all was out, God made a stay,
Perceiving that, alone of all his treasure
 Rest in the bottom lay.

For if I should (said he)
Bestow this jewel also on my creature,
He would adore my gifts instead of me,
And rest in nature, not the God of nature:
    So both should losers be.

Yet let him keep the rest,
But keep them with repining restlessness;
Let him be rich and weary, that at least,
If goodness lead him not, yet weariness
    May toss him to my breast.

                        George Herbert, *The Pulley*

3.   A bird came down the walk:
          He did not know I saw;
          He bit an angle-worm in halves
          And ate the fellow, raw.

          And then he drank a dew
          From a convenient grass,
          And then hopped sidewise to the wall
          To let a beetle pass.

          He glanced with rapid eyes
          That hurried all abroad,—
          They looked like frightened beads, I thought
          He stirred his velvet head

          Like one in danger; cautious,
          I offered him a crumb,
          And he unrolled his feathers
          And rowed him softer home

          Than oars divide the ocean,
          Too silver for a seam,
          Or butterflies, off banks of noon,
          Leap, plashless, as they swim.

                        Emily Dickinson

4.   Why, all delights are vain; but that most vain,
       Which, with pain purchased, doth inherit pain:
       As, painfully to pore upon a book
       To seek the light of truth; while truth the while
       Doth falsely blind the eyesight of his look:
       Light, seeking light, doth light of light beguile—
       So, ere you find where light in darkness lies,
       Your light grows dark by losing of your eyes.
       Study me how to please the eye indeed,
       By fixing it upon a fairer eye;
       Who dazzling so, that eye shall be his heed,
       And give him light that it was blinded by.

5.   While thus I wandered, step by step led on,
       It chanced a sudden turning of the road
       Presented to my view an uncouth shape
       So near that, slipping back into the shade
       Of a thick hawthorn, I could mark him well,
       Myself unseen. He was of stature tall,
       A foot above man's common measure tall,
       Stiff in his form, and upright lank and lean;
       A man more meagre, as it seemed to me,
       Was never seen abroad by night or day.
       His arms were long and bare his hands; his mouth
       Shew'd ghastly in the moonlight; from behind
       A milestone propped him, and his figure seemed
       Half sitting and half standing. I could mark
       That he was clad in military garb,
       Though faded yet entire. He was alone,
       Had no attendant, neither dog, nor staff
       Nor knapsack; in his very dress appeared
       A desolation, a simplicity
       That seemed akin to solitude. Long time
       Did I peruse him with a mingled sense
       Of fear and sorrow. From his lips meanwhile
       There issued murmuring sounds, as if of pain
       Or of uneasy thought; yet still his form
       Kept the same steadiness; and at his feet
       His shadow lay, and moved not.

6. Lo! where the heath, with withering brake grown o'er,
 Lends the light turf that warms the neighbouring poor.
 From thence a length of burning sand appears,
 Where the thin harvest waves its wither'd ears;
 Rank weeds, that every art and care defy,
 Reign o'er the land and rob the blighted rye:
 There thistles stretch their prickly arms afar,
 And to the ragged infant threaten war;
 There Poppies nodding, mock the hope of toil,
 There the blue Bugloss paints the sterile soil;
 Hardy and high, above the slender sheaf,
 The slimy Mallow waves her silky leaf;
 O'er the young shoot the Charlock throws a shade,
 And clasping Tares cling round the sickly blade.

      George Crabbe, from *The Village*

7. There is a kind of character in thy life,
 That to th'observer doth thy history
 Fully unfold. Thyself and thy belongings
 Are not thine own so proper, as to waste
 Thyself upon thy virtues, they on thee.
 Heaven doth with us as we with torches do,
 Not light them for themselves; for if our virtues
 Did not go forth of us, 'twere all alike
 As if we had them not. Spirits are not finely touch'd
 But to fine issues; nor Nature never lends
 The smallest scruple of her excellence,
 But, like a thrifty goddess, she determines
 Herself the glory of a creditor,
 Both thanks and use.

8. Give money me, take friendship who so list,
 For friends are gone, come once adversity,
 When money yet remaineth safe in chest
 That quickly can thee bring from misery;
 Fair face show friends, when riches do abound,

Come time of proof, farewell they must away,
Believe me well, they are not to be found,
If God but send thee once a lowering day.
Gold never starts aside, but in distress,
Finds ways enough to ease thine heaviness.

Barnabe Googe

9.   Autumn hath all the summer's fruitful treasure;
Gone is our sport, fled is poor Croyden's pleasure.
Short days, sharp days, long nights come on apace:
Ah, who shall hide us from the winter's face?
Cold doth increase, the sickness will not cease,
And here we lie, God knows, with little ease.
    From winter, plague and pestilence, good Lord, deliver us!

London doth mourn, Lambeth is quite forlorn;
Trades cry, woe worth that ever they were born!
The want of term, is town and city's harm;
Close chambers we do want to keep us warm.
Long banished must we live from our friends:
This low-built house will bring us to our ends.
    From winter, plague and pestilence, good Lord, deliver us!

Thomas Nashe

10.   For within the hollow crown
That rounds the mortal temples of a king
Keeps Death his court; and there the antic sits,
Scoffing his state and grinning at his pomp;
Allowing him a breath, a little scene,
To monarchize, be fear'd, and kill with looks;
Infusing him with self and vain conceit,
As if this flesh which walls about our life
Were brass impregnable; and, humour'd thus,
Comes at the last, and with a little pin
Bores through his castle wall, and farewell, king!

11. All Kings, and all their favourites,
       All glory of honours, beauties, wits,
     The Sun itself, which makes times, as they pass,
     Is elder by a year, now, than it was
     When thou and I first one another saw:
     All other things, to their destruction draw,
         Only our love hath no decay;
     This, no tomorrow hath, nor yesterday,
     Running it never runs from us away,
     But truly keeps his first, last, everlasting day.

       Two graves must hide thine and my corse,
         If one might, death were no divorce.
     Alas, as well as other Princes, we,
     (Who Prince enough in one another be,)
     Must leave at last in death, these eyes, and ears,
     Oft fed with true oaths, and with sweet salt tears;
         But souls where nothing dwells but love
     (All other thoughts being inmates*) then shall prove
     This, or a love increased there above,
     When bodies to their graves, souls from their graves remove.

       And then we shall be throughly blest,
         But we no more, than all the rest;
     Here upon earth, we'are Kings, and none but we
     Can be such Kings, nor of such subjects be.
     Who is so safe as we? where none can do
     Treason to us, except one of us two.
         True and false fears let us refrain,
     Let us love nobly, and live, and add again
     Years and years unto years, till we attain
     To write threescore: this is the second of our reign.

                                   John Donne, *The Anniversary*

* inmates: lodgers

12.   When the Present has latched its postern behind my
             tremulous stay,
         And the May month flaps its glad green leaves like
             wings,
       Delicate-filmed as new-spun silk, will the neighbours
             say,
         'He was a man who used to notice such things'?

       If it be in the dusk when, like an eyelid's soundless
             blink,
         The dewfall-hawk comes crossing the shades to
             alight
       Upon the wind-warped upland thorn, a gazer may
             think,
         'To him this must have been a familiar sight.'

       If I pass during some nocturnal blackness, mothy and
             warm,
         When the hedgehog travels furtively over the
             lawn,
       One may say, 'He strove that such innocent creatures
             should come to no harm,
         But he could do little for them; and now he is
             gone.'

       If, when hearing that I have been stilled at last, they
             stand at the door,
         Watching the full-starred heavens that winter sees,
       Will this thought rise on those who will meet my face
             no more,
         'He was one who had an eye for such mysteries'?

       And will any say when my bell of quittance is heard in
             the gloom,
         And a crossing breeze cuts a pause in its out-
             rollings,
       Till they rise again, as they were a new bell's boom,
         'He hears it not now, but used to notice such
             things'?

                              Thomas Hardy, *Afterwards*